The Career Confidence Toolkit for Women

An Essential Guide for Coaches, HR and Career Development Professionals

Caroline Green

trotman | t

The Career Confidence Toolkit for Women

This first edition published in 2026 by Trotman, an imprint of Trotman Indigo Publishing Ltd, 18e Charles Street, Bath BA1 1HX.

© Trotman Indigo Publishing Ltd 2026

Author: Caroline Green

British Library Cataloguing in Publication Data
A catalogue record for this book is available from the British Library.

Paperback ISBN 978-1-911724-81-0
eISBN 978-1-911724-82-7

Every effort has been made to trace copyright holders and to obtain their permission for the use of copyright material. The publisher apologises for any errors or omissions, and would be grateful to be notified of any corrections that should be incorporated in future editions of this book.

The authorised representative in the EEA is Easy Access System Europe Oü (EAS), Mustamäe tee 50, 10621 Tallinn, Estonia.

Printed and bound in the UK by 4edge Ltd.

All details in this book were correct at the time of going to press. To keep up to date with all the latest news and updates and to access the online resources that accompany this book, use this QR code or visit www.trotman.co.uk/pages/the -career-confidence-toolkit-for-women-resources

To my beautiful (inside and out) nieces

Kezia, Rebekah and Bea.

I'm so proud of the amazing women you are.

Keep shining bright.

Contents

SECTION 1: UNDERSTANDING AND OVERCOMING POTENTIAL BARRIERS

SECTION 2: UNDERSTANDING AND CELEBRATING WONDERFUL YOU

SECTION 3: ACHIEVING THE SUCCESS YOU DESERVE, NOW AND IN THE FUTURE

About the author

Caroline Green is an award-winning career development professional, learning and development specialist, and passionate advocate for women in the workplace. With nearly two decades of experience in career guidance, coaching, and CV writing, she has helped many clients to develop clarity, build confidence, and move forward with momentum. A committed Registered Career Development Professional (RCDP), Caroline is the CEO and Founder of The Talent Cycle, where she delivers career coaching, workshops, and retreats that inspire people to take control, claim their space, and own their brilliance.

Caroline's work focuses strongly on supporting women, particularly those navigating self-doubt and societal pressure, while seeking their true path. She is a visible voice for women without children, challenging assumptions and creating spaces where all women feel heard and represented. Through her female-focused events, programmes, and coaching, she brings women together to explore what confidence looks like for them, and how to move forward with purpose. She also supports organisations to help their employees grow through inclusive career development programmes and workshops.

Alongside her client work, Caroline is a dynamic presence in the career development profession, known for her energetic hosting of the first of its kind, biennial #CareersFest. An event designed to bring careers professionals and their supporters together, to celebrate, connect, learn and grow. In 2023, she was named as the prestigious Career Coach/Consultant of the Year (Private Sector) award winner by the Career Development Institute (CDI) and is a proud member of the Career Writers Association and an Associate Member of the CIPD.

She is a regular contributor to the sector's thought leadership, with writing featured in *Career Matters, Brightmine* (formerly XpertHR), and *Menopause Your Way* (QVC). Her expert insights have also appeared in national publications, including *The Sun, Harper's Bazaar*, and *In the Style*.

Her book, *The Career Confidence Toolkit for Women*, brings together practical strategies, mindset shifts, and honest reflections from years of frontline experience, combined with personal anecdotes. Aimed at career development professionals, HR teams, coaches, and women themselves, it's both a practical guide and a call to action, encouraging women to define success for themselves and take up space in their lives and careers with confidence.

Acknowledgements

They say it takes a village to raise a child, and 'birthing' a book is much the same. So forgive me a little 'Oscars speech' of thank yous to the amazing people who have helped me in this endeavour.

First, a huge thanks to Alexandra and the rest of the team at Trotman. It's so reassuring when you stick your head over the parapet and say, 'I have an idea' and you get a response of 'that sounds good'. It is wonderful to feel wrapped up in kind, supportive, highly professional, and knowledgeable arms.

Secondly, of course, a shout-out to the contributors who I introduce in more detail in the introduction, but deserve a mention here as well. Sharing your lived experience can be challenging, so I thank them all for being so open and vulnerable and helping to shape the book so beautifully.

There are also lots of other amazing women in my life who inspire me on a daily basis, including my friends, family (particularly my Mum, sisters, and nieces). I wouldn't be who I am, or in a position to write this book, without your support.

In the book, I talk a lot about how making it better for women is making it better for everyone. And conversely, many men who act as allies, who 'get it' (even when they don't), who are prepared to be the best versions of themselves and help women to be the best versions of themselves are like gold dust. And I'm lucky to have many of them in my life; you know who you are, so thank you. And to the best man of all, my darling Adrian, I couldn't do half of what I do without your help, so I thank you most of all. You can stop helping me now every time I suggest doing a variety of things or have my latest 'brainwave', responding with 'yes but you've got a book to write first' – because I've done it! Thank you, sweetheart.

Also a huge thanks to all those careers professionals, HR, coaches, mentors, and advisors who blow my mind every day with your brilliance … how often do you stop and think about the AMAZING job you do? I know lots of you will say 'often' but you're thinking about how amazing the job is. I'm not asking about that, I'm asking how often do you think about the amazing job that YOU do, how often do you take a moment to take pride and confidently own the value you add, just like we ask our clients to do? We're an empathetic, unassuming lot, but for once, take a moment to pat yourself on your back and note the great work you do. You are literally changing lives every day, supporting women (and men) to be as confident as they deserve to be and the world should thank you for that more. And a particular heartfelt thank you from me to those of you who have been so encouraging as I talked about writing this, from members of the CWA to other CDPs and in particular Polly Wiggins for your feedback and support.

To the women themselves reading this book. I know that wasn't easy. To even purchase the book, to 'admit' you want help, to say to the world you feel less than you should be, is hard. But you know what? You're stronger than you think and the world is now going to sit up and take notice of the Queen you are. Don't lose this moment, be who you were always meant to be.

And finally, the biggest thank you of all, to myself. Yes, there is a part of me that wants to cringe and the ground to swallow me up as I write that, and yet … it's our society which says we can't be confident, we can't acknowledge our greatness, we mustn't be a 'show off'. Well, sorry, but I am so over playing small, it's time to be confident, as the book shows everyone, including myself, and it would never have come to be without me. From being the CEO of The Talent Cycle, to writing a book, while juggling clients and family and all the other things you get thrown at you as a woman in her 40s, it all succeeds because of my hard work. My inner critic and I have a strong relationship (it's a daily battle) but it's time for it to pipe down.

Because the real truth? Confidence is a muscle; it needs to be exercised. Try it. And see how far you fly.

Caroline x

Foreword

Catchy 1990s book titles aside, men and women don't actually come from different planets, but it can sometimes feel like we live in different worlds. For a host of complex factors – social, political, economic, and even biological – women experience their careers differently from men.

If you work to support women and girls with their career development (in any context), then you doubtless already know this. But do you know what to do about it? The challenges and circumstances that influence women's career development can be so complex, far-reaching, and entrenched that getting to grips with how to support our clients can feel overwhelming.

So far, so intimidating – but I have good news! In this thoughtful, readable, and deeply practical book, Caroline Green has got our backs. I think it's fair to say that Caroline is a career development enthusiast, and in this book she shares her commitment, passion, and experience generously to support everyone working in this and related sectors. The book is also a valuable read for any woman considering her own personal career development – it certainly gave me plenty to think about!

As well as diving into the context that shapes women's career development, this book outlines the many and varied challenges that women face in their work. These challenges can manifest in a lack of confidence that impacts women's careers. The book explores the potential reasons behind this lack of confidence and provides solutions via a host of highly practical tools that can be used by professionals and individuals alike.

If you're a careers coach, career development professional, HR professional, or educational professional who works with women and girls of any age, this book will help you to support your clients with their careers. It is filled with insights from a host of brilliant women, entertaining personal anecdotes, and usable ideas – all communicated with Caroline's signature flair.

Since first reading this book I have used many of the tools and techniques that Caroline shares with both my clients and myself, so I have absolutely no doubt that you will find useful ideas here too. Whilst we cannot singlehandedly solve the embedded problems that women face in their careers and lives, we can support their career confidence. For many this will be helpful, but for some it can be life-changing. This is work that's worth doing, so please dive into this fabulous book as you continue to support the women and girls that you work with.

Polly Wiggins

Introduction – a powerhouse team

Maths was never my thing at school. So I'm surprising myself by starting with some calculations. Based on data from the House of Commons Library (2024), and according to my calculations, women are expected to make up approximately 48% of the UK workforce in 2025 (both part-time and full-time employees). If you're working in the world of careers, as a Career Development Professional (CDP) and/or working in HR (Human Resources/Personnel/Talent/People Management), the likelihood of you having clients or colleagues who are female is 'pretty high'. (I know, I'm a Maths genius!)

While it's important to avoid lazy stereotyping, there are common themes that women often are affected by, and need help with, in their careers.

And making it better for women is making it better for everyone.

So read on, if you're:

- A CDP or HR professional, struggling in stretched sectors where every moment counts and any information or resources at your fingertips will save you time and sanity. For the sake of continuity, I refer to 'CDPs' and 'careers professionals' a lot in the book and to be clear, I mean anyone working with young people or adults, whether that be in an educational or a work environment, employed or self-employed, with a 'careers' title or an 'HR' one. I see us all as part of one huge community, supporting others to live better working lives.
- Working with girls (perhaps in an educational setting) although I refer to 'women' in the book, so many of these challenges start practically from birth, so it's important information when working with younger females too.
- A woman trying to build her own career confidence – you'll feel the collective arms of the whole careers and HR community around you, as you coach yourself using the book.
- A man looking to understand, be an ally, and be a better CDP for your female clients.
- Part of the trans and non-binary intersex community looking for a book packed full of useful information and a safe space.

I've got you.

Don't read this book

If you're looking for a lot of theories, models, educational debate, or discussion, we will be touching on these where relevant, but really this book is a practical guide. It's about handy tips and tools, and lived experience of what really works, helping women move forward confidently in their careers and going beyond just saying 'you need to be more confident'. That doesn't work.

A book as unique as the women it serves

Each chapter will give:

- Context. What are the issues that surround, and can potentially impact, women's career confidence.
- Case studies and lived experiences of amazing women, willing to share their stories of why this all matters, and how to make it better.
- Tools. You're short on time and energy; you want to focus that on your clients, so don't spend time thinking up and designing your own tools; use these. Share the success you've had to help others' practice, using #CareerConfidenceToolkit.
- And remember … it's a practical guide, feel free to write all over it, add to the margins, pop in some Post-its. The more lived-in, the better! Some of the concepts may not be new to you, but the key is the context we're putting around them.

Amazing women

Sadly, one of the things my research has taught me is that women empowering other women doesn't always happen. It's also not just a patriarchal society but the actions and attitudes of other females, often driven as a result of that patriarchy, we have to battle with. So I'm delighted that this is not the case in this book! As well as sharing my story as a woman and a CDP, I've interviewed some brilliant women to share their journeys, of themselves and their clients. Some are passionate careers professionals and RCDPs; others are from a variety of other sectors.

And these women, amazing powerhouses that they are, are also all normal women. They're not the kind of intimidating nonsense images we see in the media; the woman running about in her high heels, with two perfectly groomed and behaved children, heading off to a three-hour Pilates session while simultaneously running her ten-figure-a-month business and doing a viral UN talk. You know the type. The ones that allegedly inspire us, but really make us want to hide under the duvet. The women here instead are real, with a story to tell, that all women are amazing; we just need to help them see that.

I wanted to introduce them, before meeting them later in the book, so in alphabetical order:

Ayo Sobo-Keane

Ayo is a commercially aware and strategically focused senior HR professional and leader. She is currently working as the Head of HR, where she balances the needs of employees with those of the business.

Charlotte Yallop

An Employment Law Partner (solicitor), with extensive experience providing strategic employment law advice to businesses. Charlotte is a passionate advocate of women's rights and co-founder of a networking group for professional women.

Cheryl Insley

An award-winning image consultant and personal stylist, Cheryl uses her skills from a previous career spent in HR to help clients navigate life transitions with confidence and clarity. Her aim is to empower women to feel confident both inside and out.

Elizabeth Willetts

Following a career in corporate recruitment, after having babies, Elizabeth needed something more flexible. Not finding it with other employers, she set up her own award-winning business helping others find flexible roles, and is also a podcaster and author.

Emily Monsell-Holden

After 20 years in marketing and comms, Emily co-founded a business to help purpose-driven businesses. She is also a mentor, podcaster and TEDx speaker, and shares her journey of working while going through fertility treatments, eventually building a life she loves, without children.

Emma Jones, MCIPD

A highly experienced HR professional and career coach, Emma has had a varied career working for other organisations and herself. She shares her personal journey with premenstrual dysphoric disorder (PMDD) and menopause.

Farrah Morgan

Farrah works with ambitious grads to help them get noticed, hired, and promoted into well-paid, inspiring careers. She runs 1-2-1 sessions and group career club programmes, supporting grads to succeed at work.

Gemma Brown

With a previous career in management in the tourism industry, an experience with a coach led Gemma to establish her own coaching business. She supports clients via coaching, workshops, and using tools like journaling.

Jo Phillips

Rising through the ranks into senior leadership in the male-dominated Recruitment and Talent sector, Jo gained first-hand insight into the barriers women face at work. Now, as Founder and MD of a movement to recognise 100,000 women in the workplace, she champions gender equity and helps women thrive both professionally and personally.

Julie Grimes

With a career history in recruitment, Julie now runs her company supporting women to deal with the effects of the menopause. She is a Certified Menopause Coach and, alongside helping individual women, advises businesses and their employees on this transition.

Kate Nash, OBE

Founder of a social business that builds disability confidence from the inside, Kate is a self-proclaimed 'agitator' and now an author. She has worked for over four decades to invite people and organisations across the world to consider 'disability' in new ways.

Katherine Jennick, RCDP

Well known in the careers world, Katherine is passionate about empowering people to recognise and celebrate all they have to offer. She is the founder of an award-winning card activity and co-architect of the #SoMuchMoreThanTalkingAboutJobs campaign.

Katherine Watkins, FCIPD, JP, BA (Hons)

Founder of an HR consultancy business, Katherine has spent her career working with corporate organisations in sectors such as banking, accountancy, and legal services. Outside work, she is a qualified Magistrate.

Lee Gilbert

After an extensive career running various companies, from marketing and web design to estate agency, in 2015 Lee sold the business and went into consulting. Aimed at giving her some time with family and focusing on her own journey, she came out as a trans woman to her family in 2015, and then professionally in 2020 alongside a new role.

Liane Hambly, RCDP

Renowned in the careers sector working with clients, training others, and a multiple-times published author. Here, Liane talks about her personal journey as part of the LGBTQIA+ community and how to support clients in that community.

Lucy Marie Hornsby

A Change and Communications Consultant, Lucy Marie has spent much of her career in the technology industry. She is co-author of a book unpacking the important topic of allyship, what it is, and why it matters so much to help women.

Mo (Mousumi) Kanjilal

Founder and Director of a business supporting others to drive inclusion, Mo has decades of experience in the corporate sector and leadership. She is also a Girls' Network mentor and TEDx speaker.

Ruth Forster, RCDP

Having left school at 16 with the world at her feet but no clue what she wanted to do, Ruth eventually fell into recruitment, loved it, and set up her own recruitment business. Alongside running this in the engineering and manufacturing industry, she is also an RCDP and volunteers as an Enterprise Adviser for The Careers & Enterprise Company.

Ruth McAteer, RCDP

A CDP based in Malaysia, Ruth's work in the careers space focuses on exclusion to inclusion, investigating how to rethink career curriculum design, resources, and events as well as traditional one-to-ones, to maximise accessibility.

Sarah West

A senior nurse with over 20 years of experience in the NHS, Sarah retrained as a certified ADHD coach. Her passion lies in supporting women who are late diagnosed with ADHD, or suspect they may have it, particularly those navigating the challenges of perimenopause and menopause.

Vanessa Cowland

A learning and talent evangelist, Vanessa has worked in a variety of senior talent roles during her career. She is currently a People Development Director and believes that women need not shy away from ambition.

Vicki Knights

A visibility strategist, brand photographer, and positive psychology practitioner, Vicki works with clients to show up and be seen with more joy and confidence. She is a firm believer in the power of personal brands and supports clients through coaching programmes, photography, and retreats.

Victoria Collins, BA (Hons), CMg MCMI, CertRP

Victoria is a business owner who has worked in the construction industry for over 20 years, gaining experience on construction projects for both private and commercial sectors. She is also a mum to two boys, a mature student, and believes that #ShowingUpIsntShowingOff.

So that's the team. Now let's get started with how we can help you and your clients.

Come on, let's do this!

SECTION 1
Understanding and overcoming potential barriers

Chapter 1
Dresses with pockets and a 'Whole Lotta History'

I'm blessed to have many wonderful women in my life, including old school friends. In Year 7, I met my first 'bestie', Hannah. Some 33 years later, she juggles her career with raising two young boys and still finds time for her friends, as displayed recently when we went on a cheeky Monday afternoon shopping trip. Heading into our first shop, the conversation went something like …

Me: 'This dress is nice.'
Hannah: 'Yes, that would suit you.'
Me: 'What's this on the side?'
Pause as I slipped my hand inside. Gasp from us both!
Both of us in joyful glee: 'IT'S GOT POCKETS!'

Yes, fellow careers and HR colleagues, there is little so special, or exciting, to women, as a dress with pockets. A fun fashion item and style choice, absolutely. But also a symbol of how far we have come.

In the 16th century, men began to have pockets sewn into trousers, but women, who had to wear skirts, did not have that luxury (Huntington, n.d.), instead having to tie small pouches onto belts. With women denied functional, easy-to-access pockets, it wasn't just about clothing; it was about limiting their ability to carry money, keys, or documents without being supervised or relying on a man. Later, as women's fashion shifted to much more restrictive clothing, there was no space for pockets, which would destroy the 'womanly shape' of the silhouettes, and so women were expected to carry small handbags. Delicate and impractical.

After all, why would they need pockets anyway? They had no money of their own; that would be managed by the father and then husband. Keys to a car or property, all under the control of the man. And it was only relatively recently that the law did anything to break the cycle.

A quick history lesson ...

- In 1928, women in the UK finally gained the right to vote on the same terms as men, removing the age and property restrictions set in 1918.
- In 1970, the Equal Pay Act made it illegal to pay women less than men for the same work, though enforcement remained weak (we'll look at whether this has actually changed, later).
- Crucially, it wasn't until the Sex Discrimination Act of 1975, however, that it became illegal for banks to deny women a bank account, loan, or mortgage based on gender or marital status. Before this, banks could legally discriminate, often requiring married women to get their husbands' permission.

Impact

You could be forgiven for thinking this is all history, so it doesn't matter now. Women, after all, *do* now own houses, bank accounts, and, of course, dresses with pockets (and yes, I did also buy the aforementioned one). But the reality is the impact of how women have been treated over the years still remains. The memory lingers, the effects are still present in society, and new ones arise, sometimes now more subtly and subliminally than in history, but the impact is still huge.

International Women's Day (IWD) 2025 had a theme of 'accelerate action' because without it, we won't achieve full gender parity for 135 years. So we are still living under the shadow of the patriarchy. When we talk about 'the patriarchy', we're referring to a social system in which men hold primary power; in roles of political leadership, moral authority, social privilege, and control of property, among other things. It's one of the walls we need to break down, as when women thrive, by having a say, we all benefit (as is the topic for IWD 2026). Because sadly, that isn't happening yet.

This might come as a surprise to hear how much women are still suffering. Why? Because if there is one thing we can do, it's internalise things. Jo Phillips, an executive coach, explains, 'Women internalise the invisible barriers that they face, and assume that the barriers are a result of their behaviours.'

With 64% of the feedback women receive being based around their behaviours (as opposed to the 1% men receive), women are often left with 'opinionated vagaries'. Where men have clear, actionable, and tangible steps to work on, and role models in more senior positions to follow, women are left feeling confused, with very few role models. As Jo puts it, this leads them to 'question if their authentic self is good enough and leading to confusion and a lack of confidence'.

Research by the Young Women's Trust shows that challenges also start early in women's careers, with the number of young women reporting a lack of progression opportunities rising from 47% to 52% (from 2022 to 2024). Even more concerning, 27% of HR decision-makers agreed it's harder for women to progress than men in their organisations, and 16% believed men are better suited to senior management roles (Young Women's Trust, 2024).

Limiting beliefs

All of this can play into the beliefs we hold about ourselves. These beliefs come from multiple factors, from our lived experiences to how we perceive societal history. We often talk about the bigger impact of these things, from shocking gender-based violence cultures to the economic impact of women not being fully utilised in their careers.

But what impact on a more personal level can this have on a woman's career and confidence? They can be left asking:

- If the law until recently said I couldn't be trusted to even manage my own finances, should I have belief in myself, my self-worth, or confidence?
- How can I make confident career moves or achieve goals when my confidence has been knocked so brutally?
- Am I just not good enough? The answer is yes, you are! But when societal past microaggressions mix with modern-day challenges that can creep in so subtly you don't spot them, it's no wonder you second-guess yourself.

- Am I being selfish if I set boundaries? With women given the lion's share of caregiving, of both children and elderly relatives, boundaries are crucial.

- What will happen if I say 'no'? For women brought up in this servient life model, often reinforced by being the main caregivers for children and elderly relatives, they believe that it isn't possible to set boundaries. But Ayo Sobo-Keane, a senior HR professional, stresses, 'It's important to set boundaries from the start. If you don't, people will learn how to push them, and that they can get away with it.'

CDPs can support clients by helping them recognise that their beliefs are not fixed; they have the agency to change them. While this concept can be challenging for some, it's crucial, as beliefs strongly influence relationships, abilities, and opportunities, all of which are closely tied to career development. Also, our beliefs are often shaped by experience, but they also shape the experiences we have. I learned this first-hand while working with a career coach during a period where I felt stuck in a negative mindset. I told her things weren't going well. She asked, *'Are they not? Or is it just your response to the situation?'*

At first, this felt dismissive, like I was being told to just 'think positive'. But with time, I realised I had more influence over the situation, and my reaction to it, than I'd originally realised.

This led me to explore Double-Loop Learning, a model by Chris Argyris (1999), which highlights how we can shift not just our actions, but the underlying beliefs driving them.

- Single-Loop Learning is about working within existing beliefs: identifying a goal, taking action, and adjusting based on feedback.

- Double-Loop Learning challenges the beliefs and assumptions behind the goal itself, asking whether they help or hinder progress.

This is particularly powerful in coaching women, whose beliefs are often shaped by social conditioning, to stay quiet, play small, or not be 'too much'.

For example, a client might say she's 'bad at presentations' and needs to improve. Rather than accepting this at face value, we can ask: is this true? Or is she holding back because she fears being seen? Is she genuinely poor at presenting, or is she simply uncomfortable being seen?

By helping clients examine these beliefs, we move beyond surface-level goals and create space for real change. As Ayo put it, 'this often doesn't come naturally to a lot of women. Being confident in your own skin often doesn't happen till you're a bit older, and you're not so bothered about what people think.' But she also reminds us, 'we're fighting against years and years of conditioning and prejudice so it's not going to happen overnight but we've got to continue'.

A tool for challenging belief systems using this method is included at the end of this chapter.

A safe space

In order to allow room for addressing limiting beliefs, CDPs need to create psychological safety. It's a term thrown around a lot, but what does it actually mean? To me, it means being free from fear. Feeling able to speak up, ask questions, share ideas, and be vulnerable, even talking about things like mistakes or worries, without worrying you'll be judged, ridiculed, or ignored. It's a cornerstone of what a good CDP provides. And for women and girls, who get judged in many ways, practically from the moment they're born, it's even more important.

A key to achieving this is to meet clients where they are. To take things at their pace, to understand you may be dealing with highly emotive and challenging topics and to be client-centred. But as Liane Hambly, renowned RCDP, points out, that can be easier said than done. She believes that we should all be thinking of 'what does being client-centred really demand from you, from your emotional resilience, of your own self-awareness. It's always a work in progress, to try and be client-centred.'

Some ways to keep striving for this include:

- Exploring the client's story without assumptions;
- Asking for and using the client's pronouns and sharing your own;
- Understanding how far they want to be stretched;
- Asking how they need you to show up for them.

These considerations are especially important during the contracting stage but equally crucial to revisit at any point.

Lee Gilbert, a trans woman and senior marketing professional, also points out that psychological safety isn't set by you; it's set by the client. 'Psychological safety is everything for someone who is trying to engage somebody. But it's an impact rather than an action. You think you're making me psychologically safe but unless I feel that way, it's not psychological safety.' She points out that we can walk into one CDP space and it feels completely different to another, so getting feedback on if we are actually creating a sense of psychological safety or not for that individual is important.

And the thing with this is, it doesn't happen overnight or in a moment; it happens over a period of time. Furthermore, another aspect of it is around vulnerability. Lee says that 'giving vulnerability to receive vulnerability often works as a playbook' and can allow people to show up as themselves. This is particularly important for women who spend their lives trying to hide their vulnerability, to protect against judgement, career disadvantage, and just basic safety.

Jo also suggests we encourage women to be comfortable with showing assertiveness. She believes there is no such thing as a 'glass ceiling' but simply 'societal expectations of female's behaviours and the backlash/bias that exists as a response to any female who chooses to assert herself using the same behaviours that she would see the male gender doing'.

Jo's LevelUp programme highlights the invisible barriers women face and educates allies simultaneously to be upstanders to support women to understand their value, encouraging organisations to recognise the barriers and for women themselves to externalise them. Demonstrating time and time again to women that 'you'd be amazed at the leverage losing you creates'.

She also suggests careers professionals read up on some of these challenges and invisible barriers, and then support women to understand their value (more on that later in the book), and encourage clients to look for opportunities both internally and externally.

The gender elephant in the room

As I touched on in the introduction, making things better for women is making things better for everyone. But at a time when talking about gender feels like a 'hot potato', why would I single out one particular gender? Am I myself discriminating? Yes, and no, is my belief. I strongly believe that as careers professionals, and frankly as decent human beings, we should never discriminate against anyone for any reason. It fundamentally goes against any kind of code of ethics we all should be following. And we should be providing a safe space for everyone, including men and non-binary people as well as trans men and women. But we need to recognise the specific challenges many cis and trans women are fighting against, some examples of which we've explored already. And in my research and conversations I've had, it has heightened the need to address these challenges; either specific to women or the unique way they deal with universal challenges.

Luckily, the tide is, however, turning, as Ruth Forster, an RCDP and recruitment specialist in the manufacturing industry, is keen to point out. 'Younger generations don't see themselves as male or female, just as people. They've come through a much more equal society, and don't see the labels we put on people.' While this is great to hear, there are still many challenges for older women and even some young people, so we need to keep up the fight for full gender parity.

Allyship

One of the ways to achieve this is in all working together. Lucy Marie Hornsby, an author on the topic of allyship, explains what that actually is. 'Being an ally is about coming in with no judgement. Asking questions, not making assumptions, understanding you're not the expert, and learning yourself.' Of course, we can all do this in our lives, but this also sounds a lot like the role of a CDP, no? Another example of the myriad of ways we can support our clients and create a psychologically safe environment. Indeed, Lucy Marie also adds that allyship is 'about being there for somebody, but not asking for recognition for it'.

Despite this, allyship is often absent in workplaces, with real consequences for women. A number of barriers get in the way:

- Cancel culture creates fear, particularly among men and older generations, about saying or doing the wrong thing. Lucy Marie explains, 'There's a fear of having privilege so I feel guilt and don't know how to show up for others. For many of the men interviewed for my book, they fear they're going to say or do the wrong thing and can't add value.'
- A re-emerging 'laddish culture' can make allyship a target for ridicule. Lucy Marie points out that 'men also get bullied over this "mate you're only sticking up for her because you want to get into her knickers" type approach'.

- In male-dominated industries, where women are often sidelined or harassed, allyship is especially important. As Lucy Marie highlights, 'allyship shows men that saying things like "your bum looks nice in that skirt" is a form of inappropriate behaviour and sexism'.

Allyship isn't only a role for men. Women, too, can show up for one another, though this doesn't always happen. Lucy Marie suggests it can include a plethora of things such as 'sticking up for them, being an advocate for them, putting them forward for work, the list is endless but it doesn't always work out that way'.

We'll explore this more later in the book, but it's worth reflecting now on how you can be an ally to women and their careers, whatever your gender. When we actively support specific groups, we contribute to making things better for everyone.

Summary

Women have faced systemic barriers throughout history. While some improvements have been made, from culture and attitudes to laws of protection, much stigma remains. And this can all leave women to fear: 'am I good enough?'

As CDPs, we can create psychologically safe environments to help women explore the external barriers they face, address their internally held limiting beliefs, and design positive career plans for moving forward. We can't change history and we can't change society, other than acting as allies, fighting against injustice, and being inclusive ourselves. But we can support our clients in establishing positive ways of interacting within a negative backdrop and forging constructive steps forward for themselves and their confidence in their careers. In the next section, we'll share some tools to help you do just that.

Tools

At the end of every chapter is a set of tools designed to help you support your female clients with smashing their confidence goals and living their best authentic lives. You might have come across some of the tools before, but think of it like an iceberg. The smaller bit above the waterline is what we see, for example, what the client says and their body language. The much larger piece underneath can be made up of everything from personal lived experience to the impact of societal expectations on women. It is this context you need to draw from to think about how these particular tools can help your female clients break down the barriers women and girls face and help them move forward successfully.

Coaching questions

So how do we do that? Questions are the answer ... whatever the question is! I personally believe that nothing really beats asking the right question, at the right time, for really helping a client. They're great to ask during career sessions, but can also be given to clients as pre-session prompts or to keep the thinking going after a session. And if you're reading this for your own self, they can be a great way to coach yourself. You can either use these as a prompt to talk with a trusted accountability partner or, as I do with many of my clients, you can use these questions as journaling prompts. We'll talk more about journaling later in the book.

So, when you're either starting to work with a new client, or perhaps you're noticing the client has some firmly held beliefs or ideas that you feel need to be explored further, these questions may help. They're all aimed at getting to the root cause of belief systems, encouraging the client to think with no barriers and also start to question whether anything might be holding them back (including themselves).

- What would you do if you weren't afraid?
- What would you do if you knew you couldn't fail?
- What is your earliest memory and how has this influenced your life? OR What are the ten most significant things that have influenced the way in which you live your life? Having a higher number like this can help dig deeper and not just give the surface-level answers. I did this activity many years ago and realised that my boundaries around work and how much I was prepared to give to another employer were not, as society might tell you, because I'm a 'lazy millennial', but really all about how I was treated in my first workplace after university.
- Who are the most important people in your life? In what ways do they help or hinder you?
- What is working well for you in your life?
- What do you expect of yourself? Is this fair? What would your best friend say about this?
- What can keep you moving forward?
- If I could grant you one wish, what would it be?

The Wheel of Anything

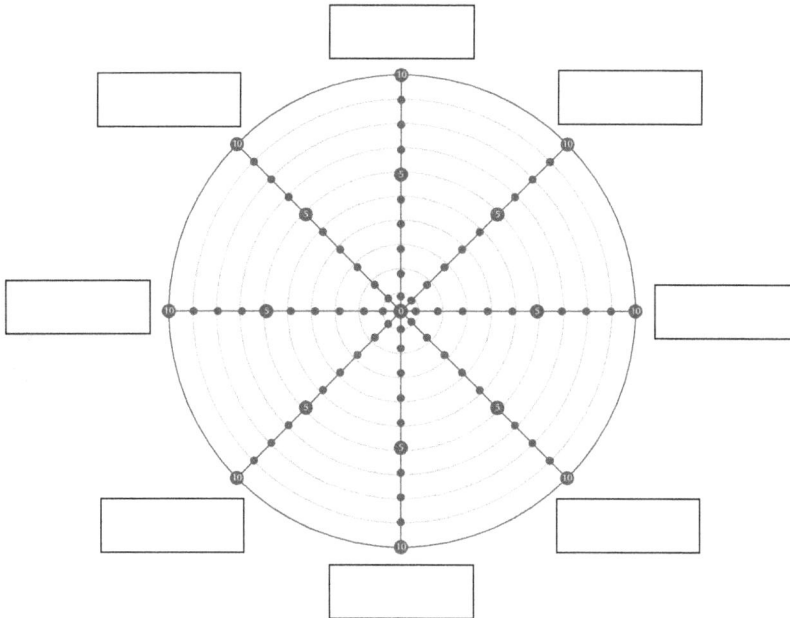

Originally known as the Wheel of Life, the now dubbed Wheel of 'Anything' is a great coaching tool to get a quick helicopter view of a topic. It's appealing to both visual learners and those with a penchant for numbers.

Wheel of Anything

The wheel has eight segments, so agree with your client what they want to allocate to each. This could be areas of their life, for example, work, home, relationships, hobbies, wellbeing, financial, health, and so on, or on something more specific, such as different aspects of a job role. Once the names have been written on the sections, ask the client to allocate a score from 0 to 10 for their confidence or satisfaction for each section, by drawing a line across each segment of the wheel. This then gives them the new outer edge of their wheel, and they can identify how balanced or not their overall wheel is, which can give some useful insights, as well as looking at each individual section.

I recently worked with a client who had just started in a leadership position and was trying to identify who she was in this new role. She was on a leadership team that was all men, and she was feeling anything but confident about this and felt she had only been offered the position as a 'token female'.

She identified eight areas the role should cover:

- Strategic design;
- Project/programme management;
- Management (people);
- Operational management (things);
- General leadership;
- Collaborating with peer group;
- Marketing what her team does inside and outside of the company;
- And she was concerned about how she would find the time for all of this, so we added time management.

When I asked her to rate from 0 to 10 how confident she felt about each of these things, a lightbulb went on. Some were given higher scores than expected, and so we could unpick that; some were directly impacted by each other, such as time management being such a struggle as she wasn't giving herself the time to feel confident about leadership. She could also see that her confidence in operational management, something she was well versed in, was becoming her security blanket, and it was actually that which was causing her time management issues. From this, she discovered that she just needed to shift her focus and realise what her new job actually required of her. With that, she could give herself more time to help build her confidence in the area of leadership. It wasn't that she wasn't capable of being a strong leader; far from what she'd been telling herself, she was just so busy caring about her team and the things she'd done in the past that she'd not allowed herself to re-focus her new priorities and let herself shine.

Another approach to this might be to just ask what areas the client would like to build confidence. It's a good way of meeting clients where they are now, and then helping them move on to where they want to be and understanding what external and internal things might have been blocking their way.

The '5 Whys?' climbing frame (double-loop activity)

This activity is all about challenging your client's thinking patterns.

1. Start by asking your client to recall a recent situation where they felt stuck, frustrated, or where things didn't go as planned. This should be something they want to change or understand better.

2. Identify the action – what did you do?

3. This is the first loop. Ask questions to help investigate and clarify the effectiveness of this, such as:

   a. What happened as a result of that action?

   b. Was that the result you wanted?

   c. If not, what result were you actually trying to achieve?

4. Now ask a series of 'why?' questions – imagine it like a climbing frame – you may go off on different tangents, but that's OK. We sometimes need to do that to understand that first loop and move on to the second. Sometimes, it's more about drilling down in a more linear fashion. Example:

   a. Why did you not apply for that role? 'I thought I'd look foolish.'

   b. Why did you think you'd look foolish? 'Because I wouldn't get it.'

   c. Why would you not get it? 'Because I don't meet all the criteria in the job description.'

   d. Why would you need to meet all the criteria? 'Because without it I don't feel good enough'.

   e. And why don't you feel good enough? 'It's just how I feel.'

5. Now is the time to challenge assumptions (double loop). Ask questions like:

   a. Where do you think that belief comes from?

   b. Is that belief always true?

   c. What is your evidence for that?

   d. Is that belief helping or hindering you right now?

6. Next up, try something new! Invite them to try a more flexible belief – you're self-aware enough to know your strengths and blind spots and what and how you need to work on them – and then try and test that belief. For extra power, work with the client to reflect back on this exercise, and after they try out the new belief, to see the impact it has had.

This activity is available as part of the online resources that accompany this book. To access, scan the QR code or visit the web address at the start of this book.

Chapter 2
Our makeup
(not the stuff we
buy in Boots)

As well as dealing with external factors, women also have to cope with what is happening internally. Yes, my friends, I'm talking the joy that is hormones. Hormones are chemicals which carry messages through a person's blood to different parts of the body. For women, oestrogen and progesterone are key, and testosterone is also important. These play crucial roles in everything from mood and general health, to bone density, pregnancy and menopause. But as much as they're technically there to help, they can hinder too.

Hormones cause physical and emotional changes and overcoming these to build confidence and thrive at work, can feel like a monumental task for women. We'll be focusing here on cis-women but remember trans people's experiences with hormones, periods, and menopause vary depending on their individual biology and medical choices, including whether they take gender-affirming hormone therapy (GAHT).

Keep quiet and carry on

The battle with hormones is deep-routed and there are many challenges, including:

- For centuries, women have been told that as hormonal cycles are natural, you just have to put up with it and carry on. Taking time off work for example feels wrong when you're not 'ill' as such. Never mind that you're doubled over in pain.

- Hormones can also have catastrophic consequences; for example, around one in ten women have experienced suicidal thoughts as a result of perimenopause (Menopause Support, 2023). Stats are even higher for certain conditions (some of which we'll explore in this chapter).
- A very personal/sensitive topic – not every woman wants to talk about their hormones (particularly in the workplace).
- Every woman is different, so even talking to another woman doesn't always garner the level of support needed.
- This can all be compounded by a medical system which doesn't seem to understand, or want to listen and take women seriously (many studies show up to a third of women face misdiagnosis of conditions like perimenopause).

It's perhaps no wonder that with this daily battle, women might not have as much energy as you'd think, when it comes to facing their careers. And the hormones are zapping the energy in themselves too.

It starts early

The impact of hormones usually kicks in for most females during their already complex teenage years; for some, hormonal changes and menstrual cycles can begin as early as age seven. Dealing with puberty, emotions, and a menstrual cycle can be a lot. Having your first period at a tender age can be a scary process, even when you've been told about it, you never really know what to expect. You're also 'battling' with friends, trying to fit in, embarrassed to share when you do start, or worried if you don't start as soon as everyone else. There is also the pain to contend with, which for some girls can be sheer agony from the start.

We can be a client's ally here. For those working within education settings, we all know timetables are tight: we don't get enough time with students and can't always see everyone we need in the allotted time. But it's our ethical responsibility to advocate for the students. If a student arrives doubled over in pain, or explains they're feeling 'hormonal' or 'emotional', this isn't the day to talk careers. Try and have other students in reserve or similar systems, so you can afford a degree of flexibility with your appointments.

Running career events in schools you can also support female students (without having to quiz them) in many ways, such as:

- Having toilets nearby (whenever I run careers events in schools, I always ensure there are student toilets nearby and a set of toilets for the exclusive use of volunteers).

- Flexibility – depending on the time of their cycle, women and girls can feel exhaustion. So ensure breaks and breakout areas throughout the day.
- Water – make sure there is water accessible, to keep hydrated and to take medication if required.
- Different ways to engage and interact with employers – at certain points in her cycle, a female may not be as chatty as normal. Sometimes, you just want to curl up and hide away. Obviously, that can't happen in the middle of a school day, but what other ways can you help, such as whiteboards as Q&A opportunities for those feeling less communicative.

Small tweaks like these show that while we are not healthcare professionals, a bit of thought and human kindness go a long way and ensure students can get the most out of the careers activity and help them advance in their career plans, which is very much within our remit!

Menstrual cycles and the workplace

Of course, it's not just teenagers who experience menstruation and its symptoms, many women also manage these while at work. A study by CIPD (2023) found that more than two-thirds of the over 2,000 women surveyed reported a negative impact on their work when menstruating. Beyond access to free period products, the study highlighted the importance of fostering a culture of awareness and support. Around half (49%) of the respondents said they wouldn't disclose the real reason for taking time off, due to concerns it would be trivialised, or because they felt embarrassed or preferred to keep it private.

So how can we as CDPs help?

- Create our own culture of awareness and support. And meet your client where they are.
- Help clients investigate companies where they may have this kind of culture – investigating things like their policies around female health.
- Also advise on options like flexible working, where working from home on certain days to help with comfortable clothes, taking medication, and the old 'desk squeeze' (hot water bottle rammed

between a desk and a painful tummy) can be managed more easily at home.

- Actively listen when working with a client – see what is not being said as well as what is said. Know when to probe a little further, and create a safe space where women can open up about any emotional or physical challenges they are experiencing. Listen without judgement; often hormonal feelings are dismissed as 'just hormones' but the feelings are very real.

- Some clients may need support in finding their voice, and campaigns like 'Just a Period' from Wellbeing of Women can help them tackle the ingrained culture of silence that still surrounds menstrual health in many workplaces (Wellbeing of Women, 2024).

The cycle within the cycle

The impact of hormones, however, does not always have to be negative. Knowledge is power. Knowing your cycle can mean you ride the power of it, and work with it not against it. If you're a woman who menstruates, you may well have felt surges of energy, productivity, clarity of mind, and even decision-making, but perhaps not linked that with phases within your cycle. If we can support women to do this, however, we can potentially supercharge their career appointments, decisions, and management.

The female menstrual cycle lasts approximately 28 days and has four distinct phases.

Phase	Hormones	Actions
Menstruation phase (usually lasts for 3–7 days)	All three hormones (progesterone, oestrogen, and testosterone) are low. Energy, focus, and productivity levels are likely at their lowest during this phase.	Focusing on sleep and rest, not taking on extra commitments at work or home if you can avoid them, are good here. Showing yourself gentle kindness and not expecting too much of yourself.
Follicular phase (starts as bleeding stops, usually lasts for 11–27 days)	Sharp rises in progesterone and oestrogen in this phase mean heightened energy, higher drive to succeed, and a good time to learn.	Pick up the complex tasks and tackle the tricky projects you've been putting off. It's also a great time for performance, efficiency, and important meetings.

(Continued)

(*Continued*)

Phase	Hormones	Actions
Ovulation phase (only takes 24 hours but the hormones involved means you can feel it for 3–4 days)	Oestrogen and testosterone peak here, giving an outward focused and proactive energy.	This is a great time for important meetings, or larger-scale events and working with others.
Luteal phase (when an egg isn't fertilised, uterus is preparing to shed)	High peak of progesterone (before falling dramatically at the end) means a calming effect, everything happening a little slower, possible PMS.	You may want to hide away with a romcom, decision-making is tricky, and working from home is a good idea.

Whether using one of the plethora of apps available, or old school pen and paper, keep a diary of symptoms so you become crystal clear on what's going on internally vs externally. Then plan accordingly, instead of using outdated time/workload techniques, use your feminine powers. CDPs can help through:

- Explaining this concept with clients and working with them to plan.
- We can't always stop the world of work as it doesn't fit with our cycle, but helping clients to craft their message of when might be optimum timings for particular things can help.
- Reactive work may not be possible to change, but support clients with proactive changes they can make. For example, scheduling meetings they do control, at the best time in their cycle, or building in buffer times when decision-making will be challenging.
- Productive challenge – if a client is struggling to make career decisions, is this the best time of the month to attempt this?
- Women have to 'play the game' at work harder than men. While no woman should ever have to hide away because of their period, understanding which days are better suited to working from home in comfortable clothes with a hot water bottle, and which are best for power suits and driven development conversations with their boss, can be empowering. CDPs can help them plan this.
- Being client-centred doesn't mean a set approach for that one client. You need to flex to meet their needs. Understand that some days your female client could be full of energy and discussion, others lower in energy and mood, and so a journaling activity might suit them better.

- Don't forget that women are more than 'just' their hormones, and we've been ridiculed for them our whole lives. So tread carefully. The suggestions here require thoughtful contracting and psychological safety. They may also be things you never discuss but just have in the back of your own mind when choosing activities to support your client. There are also ways you could approach this in a more neutral way, for example, asking, 'What's your energy like today?'
- Self-reflection – if you're supporting clients while working through your own menstrual cycle, think about how that might effect how you show up and how you can manage your practice accordingly.

More than 'normal' pain

Every woman is different, so no such thing as 'normal' per se, when it comes to hormones, there are some conditions, however, where there are likely to be increased challenges.

Some of these have been publicised through high profile cases, such as that of BBC journalist Naga Manchetty. She was diagnosed at age 47 with adenomyosis, a condition in which the inner lining of the uterus breaks through the wall of the uterus. This can lead to symptoms such as heavy or prolonged menstrual bleeding, severe menstrual cramps, chronic pelvic pain, and bloating. Treatment options range from pain management and hormone therapy to hysterectomy in severe cases.

Naga has spoken about suffering debilitating pain and feeling as though she was dismissed by medical professionals. One of the key challenges women face with these kinds of conditions is being taken seriously, often dismissed as nothing serious, just need to 'woman up' and get on with it. That message is so ingrained in our psyche it can be incredibly challenging to get over, even for 'normal' period pains, where we've been told it's not an illness, get on with it, despite it feeling like your stomach is being hit by a hammer and your ovaries squeezed like an old rag, we have to show up and perform. CDPs can support their clients here, encouraging them to advocate for themselves at work, building their confidence, even to be brave enough to call in sick or explain the adjustments they need.

Likewise, there are many other conditions which can have debilitating effects, such as endometritis. This is a chronic medical condition in which tissue similar to the lining of the uterus grows outside the uterus, often on the ovaries, fallopian tubes, and other pelvic organs. This tissue acts on the menstrual cycle by thickening, breaking down, and bleeding, but with no way to exit the body. Symptoms include everything from severe menstrual cramps to fertility problems. CDPs are not medical professionals but can support clients with how they can manage the condition at work. Much like with other conditions such as adenomyosis, this could include anything from how to speak to potential employers about it, to assessing adjustments needed.

PMDD (premenstrual dysphoric disorder)

We all have those clients that stick with you. When Emma Jones, MCIPD, approached me three years ago for some career coaching, I was flabbergasted. Emma was running her own career coaching and CV writing business, and I'd admired her from afar. Like many other women, those imposter thoughts and feelings are often very real (more on that later) and I wondered 'why me?' when she approached me. Running her first session it became apparent that while she was in my view, every bit as fabulous as I thought, I wasn't sure she felt the same about herself.

She was very open about hormonal struggles and we quickly adapted to fit in with those. The main adaption, was picking session times carefully, as for two weeks of every month, she felt she wouldn't have the energy or emotional capacity to cope with a session. Emma explained at the time that she thought she might be peri menopausal and so she was one of the first women I thought of to interview for the book. It was only when we met for her book interview that it became clear there was a lot more to her situation.

Emma explained that perimenopause symptoms had been made worse by having the condition PMDD. She explained, 'It's premenstrual dysphoric disorder. And there's lots of ideas about what it is, and how it manifests itself. But my own take on it is that I am allergic to my own progesterone. So when that spikes in my cycle it means I feel quite unwell for two weeks of every month, both physically and mentally. I guess the worst thing about it is that you can feel suicidal. The way you react to things and respond, you just sort of change as a person, and that can be really hard.'

Like many other hormonal-related conditions, it can change depending on a variety of conditions, such as age, pregnancy, peri/menopause, and be affected by things such as stress. But a theme for the book is that women internalise how they are feeling and just cope. Emma agreed, saying, 'Although it can be debilitating, I've never asked for time off or adjustments. But it has had a massive impact on my confidence and my self-esteem. Because, it's a bit of a cycle that you go through with it. You behave in a certain way, then you feel incredibly guilty about it. You're not responding rationally to things.' And this thought cycle can have catastrophic results, as statistics for women with PMDD taking their own lives are very high. Emma felt that if she was 'going to bang the drum about anything, it's going to be for employers or careers professionals to know more about that'.

There is no suggestion that a CDP or HR professional should be quizzing individual women on their personal medical issues, but having an awareness of these conditions can help. If then any client does raise this with you, you know a little about what that might involve for them and what that might mean for their career. As ever, however, don't make assumptions; always make the appointment client-centred. But having an awareness of typical conditions like this, and asking how they'd like you to make adjustments for that, such as picking a time to see them during the better half of the month for them, is a small change which can have a significant impact. Not only does this make for a more productive careers meeting itself, you can also flex this knowledge to work with the client about finding the right career fit for them, given the challenges they face.

(Peri)Menopause

As well as specific conditions, like those mentioned above and pregnancy, there is also the more universal transition of perimenopause and menopause. Something which had been suffered quietly, alone, unspoken, has now been opened into conversation by the likes of Davina McCall et al. And yet, although many of us are more aware than ever before about perimenopause and menopause, there still remains lots of mystery and confusion. Stigma abounds and confidence levels have been rocked, both by the hormonal storm internally and the societal impact externally. This is something CDPs need to be mindful of.

As well as those in the workplace who've been through it when it was rarely discussed, and certainly not at work, for those of us who've heard it spoken of more, it can still be confusing. I thought I was pretty clued up. Then a hospital dash to A&E with suspected sepsis changed everything. Thankfully I didn't have sepsis, 'just' a difficult kidney infection, followed by two nightmare months where ongoing symptoms confused everyone. Some of which were side effects created by some of the medication I had been (in some cases incorrectly) given, others were baffling to everyone. In hindsight, my main symptoms were anxiety and panic over every little thing. A conversation at the time with my sister made me realise that my having always been anxious was not in fact true. A deep thinker, sure. Sensitive, definitely. But the anxiety was new. Strike one for perimenopause.

For Emma, the uncertainty around what was actually happening was part of the challenge. 'The earlier symptoms I'd had then developed into anxiety and brain fog as the years went on. And just not feeling with it, and doubting myself a lot as well. Then not being able to put names to faces and forgetting really easy words. Which was actually quite frightening, it was like, have I got dementia? And other random symptoms, like tinnitus and cold feet.'

The thing with (peri)menopause, is often it sneaks up on you. We know it's coming, but we don't always prepare for it. Only looking back, counting up the symptoms (it's not all just hot flushes and mood swings), do some realise what is happening. Sadly, the medical world commonly doesn't seem to be any more clued up either. For me, it took three appointments with different GPs (one of whom was allegedly my GP surgery's menopause expert) to actually be heard. The problem was, despite my many symptoms (including anxiety, hot and cold flushes, aching limbs, restless legs, feeling like things were crawling on me, period changes, insomnia, emotions ranging from tears to pure rage and back to anxiety again), in my early 40s, I was deemed too young and dismissed out of hand. Likewise Emma felt that 'it's been a struggle, trying to get the right advice, get the right treatment'.

For Julie Grimes, now a menopause coach, things also crept in. 'I was 45 when I really started having symptoms. My periods were getting wider apart; you think this could be menopause, but then you think you're fine. But then the periods could also be overwhelmingly heavy, really scary sort of stuff. And I had been running a really successful business, and now was anxious about decisions.'

Many of these lesser-known symptoms can have a huge impact on women and their confidence, not only in and of themselves, but questioning why it is happening. Julie points out that 'there are hundreds of symptoms but 34 main ones'. And for lots of women, taking a deep breath and carrying on is the norm. For Julie though, it got to a point where she felt HRT (Hormone Replacement Therapy) was the answer. 'I decided not to take it to start with, there had been so much scaremongering about it. But when I hit a particular low point at age 51, I started. It wasn't an automatic silver bullet, but now I feel fantastic, I've lost the weight and my mind's back. And if you don't want to take HRT there are non-HRT alternatives out there; however, making lifestyle changes like diet and exercise and reducing stress in your life is crucial to managing this time of your life.'

It's also important to note that if you're working with a woman going through the menopause process, HRT is not necessarily an automatic fix. For many women, you end up feeling like a guinea pig, trying different HRT options until you hopefully find your right 'fit'. And the journey of menopause, even with HRT, is not a two-year one, more like a ten-year one where things will ebb and flow and for those taking HRT, there is a constant battle in the mind of the help it could provide vs the associated dangers. This can knock confidence further, particularly when you hear stories of other women finding HRT so helpful. So showing clients patience and understanding, not assuming if they share they're on HRT that all will be well, is important. And Julie points out that 'unless you're seeing a BMS (British Menopause Society) approved GP, they're not always 100% sure on how to deal with menopause'.

While not a clinical study, Julie's and Emma's experiences are common, as many actual studies do show. The transition can be traumatic, from how the hormones actually effect you to what menopause means. For some, a sad goodbye to their childbearing years, for others, like me, it just made me feel really *really* old. For CDPs, our role is not to attempt any kind of therapy, but having an understanding of what your female client could be going through is important.

Impact on career confidence and how CDPs and HR can help

So if we're focused on clients' careers, why do menopause and other hormone-related conditions matter? A study by The Menopause Charity found that around 10% of women leave their jobs due to the impact of perimenopause (The Menopause Charity, 2023). This not only affects the individuals involved but also has wider implications for the economy and society.

For many, this statistic won't come as a surprise. Julie described the impact it had on her career in recruitment where she'd been 'used to going into companies selling myself at board level. Then I was questioning my decisions, worrying if I'd picked the right candidates. From being clear-minded and multitasking, my brain became muddled and that affected my energy. It became quite debilitating and I was unable to get through my to-do list and felt like I was no good at what I did, so lost my confidence.'

The process of (peri)menopause also happens at a time of life when there are lots of other pressures on women, from raising children to managing the health of elderly parents, and trying to juggle a mid-point in their career. It's a lot. Emma points out, 'it's important to remember you're not alone' so not only is it a case of finding your tribe, perhaps connecting with other women on the same journey, seeking support on the career aspect is also crucial as it can be an incredibly confusing time. Emma felt that perimenopause definitely impacted her decisions on where and how she worked, and she changed her career path based on how she was feeling. 'I realised starting a business at this point wasn't such a good idea. I had heightened imposter syndrome and said no to things I could have said yes to. I had lots of flexibility so that was good in some ways, to help with the two weeks I couldn't work but bad in others. I almost had too much flexibility so would procrastinate. I needed more structure.'

How can CDPs, HR, and businesses help?

From my experience of working with clients, and advice from Emma and Julie, there are many ways that you can make things easier for women in this transition, including:

- Many studies show flexible work is the most critical support for managing menopause symptoms. After an article I wrote on this, a well-known careers company shifted its working pattern so Careers Advisers were doing more days in schools but half days of appointments to help the energy levels of their employees. CDPs can help their clients to advocate for themselves on this and other ways which will support them.

- As always it's not one size fits all – symptoms and how an individual wants to manage them vary, so being client-centred is as always crucial. And remember symptoms can vary on an almost hourly basis.

- Time to breathe – support and encourage female clients to take time out for themselves to understand what is happening to them. For HR in particular, being aware of symptom management – clinical and non-clinical routes and signposting individuals is useful, as is awareness programmes. As we've seen, it can often creep up on you and so sometimes it's about helping to educate the person who has it. And include information on advocating for yourself included in that awareness/support package, such as 'top tips' for how to speak to a GP about it.

- Work with clients as the career that worked for 20-year-old them might not work for 40–50-plus-year-old them. They've likely still got a number of years ahead in their career so support them with next steps that fit this 'new' version of themselves. Julie also highlighted that you're forever changed after the menopause, so having a CDP to help you learn what you love about work and how to thrive is beneficial.

- Research – you're not a medical expert but an awareness of symptoms can be good for CDPs, HR, and line managers. Also promoting openness and transparency, so difficult conversations around the topic, and even asking for help, becomes less of a big deal. However, tread lightly – ensure talking about adjustments doesn't sound like judgement or failure.

- Businesses can also hire menopause experts like Julie, who can advise on what's happening and why, as well as practical tips for managing symptoms. Get everyone in these talks, including men and CEOs, so they understand there is a business argument for supporting women as well as a moral one, as it helps with a number of things including staff retention.

- As well as advising clients that these are the things they should look out for in potential employers, think also of your own careers organisation and whether you are providing all the support you can for your own staff.

Summary

Throughout her life, any girl or woman is at the mercy of her hormones. These can impact females physically, mentally, and emotionally. This can affect everything from a woman's energy levels, to the decisions she makes, to how she feels about her work. And more importantly, how she feels about herself.

As CDPs we can support clients by having background knowledge of hormone-related conditions and working with our clients to find their inner confidence. We'll be looking at many more ways to do that in the coming chapters.

Tools

We can't do anything about hormones, but we can support clients in managing some of the things hormones affect, such as ability to make a decision. These tools can be used in a variety of ways, and may help clients to see things from different perspectives.

Coaching questions

These questions in particular could be useful to help women identify where the challenges are: are they down to hormones or is it other things draining their energy and how do they want to move forward in this next phase in their life if they're going through a hormonal transition phase?

- What does happy mean to you?
- What things do you want to stop doing? What gets in the way of you stopping?
- What would you tell a friend in your situation?
- What one thing could you change to make your situation feel more positive?
- What or who drains your energy? What can you do to solve this?
- What is it that you truly want?

Knowledge is power

Whether it's fully understanding symptoms and the impact of them to go to the GP with, or having a better sense of self so you can work *with* yourself instead of against, knowledge is power. In busy life, how often do women, in particular, ever stop and assess what's really going on? A simple act of keeping a diary can be helpful or why not work with your clients to review each week and ask:

- What went well for you this week?
- What challenges did you face, and how did you overcome them or learn from them?
- How effectively did you manage your time?
- Did you stay aligned with your plans for the week?

They may also like to note other things, including how emotional they felt (happy, sad, tearful, etc.), how they slept, other physical symptoms they have noticed, and so on.

The idea of these questions as well as understanding better can be a basis of challenging thoughts. Over time do they see patterns such as more negative thinking or more productive times? What does this tell them about hormones vs 'true' thought and how can they manage that with their schedule? This can be done via discussion, or try journaling as a tool (see chapter 6 for more instructions on how to do this).

Dig a little deeper

Many women of a 'certain age' are juggling a lot. From caregiving responsibilities of their own children alongside caring for elderly relatives, with fluctuating hormones to increased work responsibilities, it's a lot. This worksheet encourages them to see what is gaining them energy, and what is draining it. Identifying these helps put them back in the driving seat, so they can then decide what to do next.

	Gains What needs to happen to gain energy from this situation?	Drains What needs to happen to drain my energy with this situation?
Type of work		
Structure of work (including flexibility)		
Meaning of work		
Quantity of work		
Relationships with people at work		
Relationships with people in personal life		
Work/life balance		
Home-life		
Family responsibilities		
Wellness – rest, exercise, health, diet, etc.		
Hormones/cycles		

This table is available as part of the online resources that accompany this book. To access, scan the QR code or visit the web address at the start of this book.

Self-care

Women often feel they just have to power through, no matter what. But 'rest is a performance behaviour' (my favourite saying ever!), so how are clients doing that? If self-care is being neglected, use a Wheel of Anything to log what that could look like or ask questions like:

- What could you add to a self-care list for you? Remember this is what works for you – meditation and sound-baths might be bliss for some, but agony for others, who'd prefer taking their motorbike out on the open road. Do you.

- What do you need to change to care for yourself like you deserve (and as you would someone else)?

- For many of us, time is what holds self-care back. What can you stop, start, do more of or less of, to help create some room for your self-care (see worksheet below)? Remember, if you don't make time for your wellness, you'll be forced to make time for your illness.

I also find this can be helpful when working with outplacement clients, planning what their 'job search project' looks like and making sure that self-care activities are included.

I need to stop:	*I need to start:*
I could do more of:	*I could do less of:*

This table is available as part of the online resources that accompany this book. To access, scan the QR code or visit the web address at the start of this book.

The done list

Using the GROW (Goal, Reality, Options, Will) model of coaching can be super helpful when it comes to hormones.

Looking at 'Options' encourages a woman who is being sabotaged by hormones to reflect on what options there *could* be. Encouraging this process without judgement or instantly shutting down ideas can free them from a hormonally charged negative mindset.

Looking at what they 'Will' do can be telling. A short list may show low energy levels, an overly long one might suggest unrealistic expectations. Or an extension of this, to help them manage that long list, is to also ask the time management question …

Is there anything they can:

- Do (now)?
- Defer/Delay (do it, just not RIGHT NOW – perhaps do at a more hormonally appropriate time)?
- Delegate (give it to someone else)?
- Delete/Ditch/Dump (do you really need to do it at all)?

But my favourite list of all with clients is to work on their 'done list'. Encourage them to reflect back on the past week, and then write a list of all the things they have **done**, however big or small. We're often so busy looking at what we've got left to do, we forget to acknowledge and celebrate how much we have already done. And if it's a week where there isn't a lot on that list, or the main point is that they 'simply survived' that week, then celebrate that too. Also unpick whether the lack of completed tasks is due to anything hormonal, and whether the client just needs to give themselves a bit of a break about that.

Chapter 3
Additional barriers
... or are they?

At The Talent Cycle, I work with organisations on organisational development and talent management strategies. Recently, an HR Director and I discussed the impact of equity on the work we were doing. Equity is often confused with equality but is fundamentally different.

Equality means treating everyone the same. Equity means adjusting to individual needs to create a level playing field (meaning where no one has an unfair advantage). If Goldilocks' three bears all wanted to sit at a table, equality would give them each the same size chair: too tall for one, too small for another, and just right for the third. Equity means providing chairs of varying sizes that fit each perfectly, so everyone can sit comfortably. This shows why equity is key to true inclusion.

Inclusivity and equity go hand in hand. Inclusivity means creating environments where everyone feels safe, respected, and able to participate fully. Equity ensures those environments adapt to remove individual barriers.

Dr William E Donald, Careers Researcher, is often the reason I go onto LinkedIn. His consistent messaging about what it means to live in a world that isn't inclusive speaks to my soul. That might sound odd as this book is for women, but it's another example of trying to create a level playing field by understanding the needs of particular individuals, which is actually what Will advocates for too.

He once shared a brilliant story of how his daughter changed a game they were playing to make it more inclusive (as Will uses a wheelchair and couldn't reach as far as his daughter in their throwing game). In doing so, she made the game more fun for both of them. Inclusivity is literal child's play, and yet we see it missing from the workplace so often.

That's why inclusivity is central to my work, whether through #CareersFest (see www.careersincareers.co.uk), an inclusive event celebrating careers professionals, or creating safe spaces for clients, tailored to their needs. CDPs and HR have a crucial role to play in making things more inclusive, not just for the success of a careers appointment but in helping clients move forward successfully in their careers. This could be for every woman, but also acknowledging those who may require accommodations or have additional needs. We'll be focusing in this chapter on a few of these, and how we can support:

- Women who may require accommodations or have additional needs (including those with physical disabilities or who are neurodivergent);
- Women of colour;
- The LGBTQIA+ community.

Disability

Often, it's not a disability itself that creates the barrier, but society itself. Ruth McAteer, an RCDP based in Malaysia who lost her hearing in her 40s, feels much of the problem is down to ableism. She describes this as 'discrimination against people with disabilities, often assuming they are less capable or inferior. It can be unintentional but just as damaging. I have a high level of self-efficacy but I still get told "You present well for a Deaf person", "... obviously you can't do that as you're Deaf". It is too common in the workplace that I have limitations put on me by others that I do not put on myself.'

Kate Nash OBE, disability rights champion, agrees, saying, 'You get the most bizarre questions and the biggest barrier is we often internalise that. It takes herculean efforts of confidence, to picture yourself having a promotion or in a more senior position. It's "other people's stuff" having a bigger impact on your own confidence.'

What we do know is CDPs and HR can help readdress the balance through:

- Creating a safe environment going forward, where women feel comfortable speaking up.
- Accepting we don't have all the answers, but we will do all we can to help.
- Creating the right environment, from setting closed captions on video calls, to ensuring offices have wheelchair access.

- Remembering, while you should offer this for any one individual anyway, it actually affects more of your clients and colleagues than you might realise. Kate highlights that 'at least 20% of most audiences will be individuals with lived experience of disability'.

- Also keep in mind that employment rates are lower among disabled people compared to non-disabled people, and there are slightly more disabled men than women in employment (ONS, 2023). Therefore, supporting our female clients is crucial.

There are also many other ways disability meets gender, and the impact of that. For Kate, she felt her experience of disability is 'so profound that it overrides other aspects like gender. And yet … the specific challenges that gender have played impacts on confidence; it impacts on ability to enter conversations and on your perception of other people's perception of you.'

Likewise, during recruitment, data tells us women already struggle with the confidence to apply for a role if they do not meet a significant proportion of the criteria, and Ruth believes for those with disabilities, they 'may feel they need to meet 100% or be overqualified to compensate for required accommodations. They feel the weight of proving their capability and overcoming inherent bias expressed as ableism.' Kate also adds that there is a sense of isolation and loneliness, without support, when 'being a woman seeking out a successful career, with the aspect of disability layered on top, and the soft bigotry of low expectation, can have a more deleterious impact on how you feel about yourself and therefore your work journey'.

So how else can CDPs and HR help? Ruth feels that HR should complete ableism training and gain feedback from female disabled employees. Luckily, a model for this already exists, thanks to the tireless work of Kate et al. She explains, 'Employee Resource Groups (ERGs) are networks mostly comprised of individuals with lived experience of disability, neurodivergence or mental ill health. Their purpose is 1) to support the business improve policy, practice, and procedure and help the business learn directly from their employees and 2) provide a fantastic source of support for how to navigate the working world, for example, how to ask for a workplace adjustment.'

A great resource, but I of course asked Kate if they included careers professionals, and sadly she didn't think they always do. This is a great opportunity for CDPs working in businesses to support, but what else can we do? Supporting our female clients, encouraging them to speak about how they feel and not internalise things, working with them to understand all their strengths and skills (see chapter 7), and helping them to investigate if a potential employer has the right culture to support. This could include:

- Are they a member of the disability confident scheme (there are three levels) or part of the Valuable 500 or a member of PurpleSpace?
- Do they have an active ERG, a disability forum, or do they have a disability network? You can often get this from the DEI part of their website. If not, are they willing to start one?
- What does the advert/application process say about their approach to disability and/or the interview process, and are they living the values they say they follow?
- Check if this is an environment where they can thrive – will the employer act or just say they will? Sometimes legal advice to check over contracts and all accommodations required are guaranteed is a helpful additional step.

It is a personal choice whether to disclose disability at interview, but Kate felt particularly that for those with visible disabilities, it can be worth addressing. 'Talk about your workarounds; assimilate it as part of your brand that makes you a really good bet, a great piece of talent to unleash into the organisation.' For a lighter touch, you can talk about the lived experience of disability, both online and in person. CDPs can help clients work through the complexities of this and decide what is the best approach for them.

A way to help develop their brand further, Ruth also suggests those with disabilities should embrace their 'worth and value, surround yourself both personally and professionally with people who uplift and celebrate you'. And one of those can, of course, be a CDP. Ruth believes that being an ally is crucial, and that 'inclusion is everyone's responsibility, and together we can engender meaningful change'.

Other needs

Aside from physical disabilities, you'll have many clients who have other additional needs or accommodations required, some of which you may not be able to see. For example, there is an estimated 15%–20% of the global population considered neurodivergent and unemployment rates among neurodivergent adults reported to be as high as 30%–40% (Mydisabilityjobs, 2024). As part of your reflective practice, you may wish to consider how inclusive an environment you are creating and do research into whether that includes those who are neurodivergent. Here, we'll just be focusing on ADHD, as in recent years, many women, in particular, are receiving late diagnoses of this as much was misunderstood about ADHD generally, and how it can show up in women. It's important we understand how this can affect their career journeys, particularly if they've spent years without the right support or recognition.

ADHD is a neurodevelopmental condition that affects the brain's executive functions, which can include the regulation of attention. People with ADHD may be easily distracted, forgetful, impulsive, or struggle with staying focused, especially on tasks that aren't stimulating. As with many conditions, it varies depending on the individual, so we need to be client-centred in our approach.

Sarah West is a qualified nurse and ADHD coach. She highlights that while for many years it has been seen as a 'boys' condition', that's not actually the case. She highlights that 'in boys, ADHD is more often associated with externalising behaviours: hyperactivity, impulsivity, and physical restlessness. In girls, it often shows up as the inattentive type, and in more internalised ways: difficulty concentrating, perfectionism, emotional sensitivity, and low self-esteem.'

Perhaps another example of society telling females to be quiet, to keep small, girls with ADHD become 'expert "maskers", covering up their difficulties to fit in socially or meet expectations. This can lead to exhaustion, anxiety, or later burnout'. It's also the start of a long journey for many women where symptoms can be mistaken for anxiety, depression, or even personality traits. This can lead to late diagnosis, which is becoming more common as we become more aware of symptoms. Sarah agrees, highlighting that late diagnosis in women often happens during transitions including pregnancy and perimenopause, where 'hormonal changes can worsen symptoms, bringing them to light for the first time'.

This delay in diagnosis can mean years of feeling 'not good enough' or wondering why things seem harder for them compared to others. Sarah also believes that ADHD can have a significant impact on confidence in the workplace, including:

- Inconsistent performance – brilliant one day, struggling the next – leading to self-doubt;
- Struggling with time management and prioritising tasks or remembering deadlines;
- Not coping with workplace noise;

- Struggling with multitasking;
- Feedback from managers may focus on what is going wrong, rather than strengths – over time, this can be internalised and lead to low self-esteem and fear of failure or imposter thoughts and feelings;
- Decision-making struggles – flitting between procrastination and impulsivity.

And Sarah concludes that particularly when undiagnosed, 'women often feel they're not living up to their potential, which can feel frustrating and isolating'.

So what can we do to ensure that our female clients with ADHD do indeed thrive? Sarah believes that you can start by looking out for three key things:

1. ADHD often looks different in females.
    Many are missed or misdiagnosed, especially those with the inattentive type. They may be overthinking, people-pleasing, masking, or experiencing anxiety.

2. Self-doubt is a major theme.
    Many of these women have internalised years of feeling 'not good enough' or 'too much'. This can impact their ability to recognise their strengths, make confident career choices, or advocate for themselves in the workplace.

3. Masking leads to burnout.
    Women with ADHD often become experts at 'coping' through perfectionism, overworking, or people-pleasing. This isn't sustainable, and by adulthood, many are exhausted and burnt out.

After this, CDPs and HR can proactively help females with ADHD in a number of ways:

- Open conversations: Foster an inclusive environment where conversations about mental health can happen. Once again, this is about creating a sense of psychological safety. This can be covered in a variety of ways, from including this in the contracting stage to posters about it on your careers room wall.
- Know the law: Offering reasonable adjustments and/or being aware they can request those at interview and in the workplace. Also provide support with Access to Work applications, which is a scheme that can help you get or stay in work if you have a physical or mental health condition or disability.

- Client-centred: Recognise that neurodivergent qualities are strengths, not deficits but know how to relay that. I often see people offer a blanket comment of 'it's your superpower' but especially for women who may be struggling with a recent diagnosis, it can feel anything but. Sarah suggests focusing on the fact that 'ADHD individuals often bring creativity, passion, problem-solving abilities, and out-of-the-box thinking'. These are all crucial skills in the recruitment process and workplace itself.

Challenges for women of colour

As well as those with disabilities and additional needs, there are other factors which can result in additional challenges for some. Women of colour, for example, can face specific challenges due to the intersectionality of race and gender. Mo (Mousumi) Kanjilal, Founder and Director of a diversity and inclusion company, agrees. She felt some of the challenges she has faced in her career were both down to her gender and her race.

These challenges manifest in many ways, including:

- Microaggression and unconscious bias.
- More overt bullying.
- Isolation and tokenism.
- Women are often underrepresented in leadership roles, and women of colour even more so. This has a variety of impacts, including a lack of role models, mentors, and sponsors.
- Lack of development opportunities remains a key issue, with one study showing that 71% of Black women, 70% of Hispanic women, and 70% of Asian women would consider leaving their workplace due to limited access to professional development (Fair Play Talks, 2022).

Mo herself experienced many of these. 'I was working in big tech companies where there were not many women or people of colour. People would ask strange things, ask if I was having an arranged marriage, couldn't say my name, would mix me up with another Indian lady (even though we didn't look alike). I could see how people perceived me and talked to me.'

For many, this can chip away at their confidence. For some, that also produces a secondary behaviour of feeling like they have to be perfect, that they're not good enough, or that they simply have to go that extra mile just to try and get on a level playing field. Mo certainly took this approach and saw great success as a result. 'When visiting clients, they thought I was there to take the minutes. But I outsold all my older, White, male peers and became vice president of sales and marketing of a 95 million pound revenue department.' A fantastic success story, but at what cost, particularly when Mo shares the struggles of everything from having to work longer hours than everyone else to dealing with bullying from colleagues and associates in professional bodies.

It's perhaps no surprise that data shows alarmingly high statistics of unemployment for women of colour. Without Mo's resilience, getting on in the workplace can be particularly challenging. So how can CDPs and HR help? Firstly, we can all call things out when we see racism happening. We can also provide welcome and inclusive spaces and be aware of things that might possibly help a female client of colour. Mo felt that if you can connect with other women, particularly those of colour, 'that solidarity is good and has helped me too'. Once again, CDPs can help here, helping clients to find their tribe and look for a company culture that fits, which is crucial to confidence and success at work. Supporting clients to think about and build their network is an activity which will see dividends whether it's within or outside of the company.

It's also important to acknowledge the positives, as well as the barriers, helping clients with building blocks for a better future. We'll look later at the importance of clients tapping into their uniqueness and what makes them, them. And Mo was given advice along the same lines, where someone said, 'You already stand out; make the most of that as in sales you want people to remember you.'

In addition to helping clients celebrate themselves, CDPs can also help with raising awareness. As Mo highlights, 'Like many Indian families, my family understood careers like medicine, law, and engineering. But I was more creative, interested in English, but had no real role models that helped me navigate that.'

I've walked this tightrope many times, particularly when working with young women, whose family and culture lay certain expectations on their career path, whether they agree or not. As CDPs we can respectfully challenge this, explore whether it is what the client truly wants, but also know when to step back. As with all clients, we shouldn't make cultural assumptions and also understand that families can be challenging, whatever your culture! They're the centre of our universe, and the thing most likely to cause stress. They can be challenging, often messy, especially for women who often feel the brunt of familial challenges, but it's the clients' prerogative of whether they want to follow in their family's wishes or not. Our role is to make sure they are aware of their options, and then support them whichever path they choose.

Other challenges — for the LGBTQIA+ community

While personal life should have no impact on careers, sadly that's not always the case, particularly if you are part of the LGBTQIA+ community. For Lee Gilbert, a trans woman, while outwardly it looked like a highly successful career journey, inwardly it felt anything but. She explains, 'When I was doing a lot of speaking, I believe in some ways my sex assigned at birth was possibly an advantage. I had formed muscle memory of all the societal expectations from tone of voice to body language and was a successful speaker. But that's part of the challenge of a gender journey. You're following the societal norms but there is an inner conflict.' That meant that while Lee had known from age seven that there 'was something', it wasn't until 2015 she came out as trans to her family, and 2020 professionally. She says, 'In 2020 it was quite euphoric, as for the first time I was my whole self professionally.'

Aside from the initial euphoria, Lee also felt that the journey has taught her about being, and showing, her vulnerability and her authentic self. But the journey hasn't always been smooth. 'I've been blessed that I developed personal confidence, pre-transition. That did take a dip initially after however, I became overly conscious of how to express that confidence as a trans woman, questioning if how I was acting was authentic or muscle memory.'

So how can CDPs help clients who are dealing with some of these challenges? Lee felt that there is a need to 'create an environment that is persistent and consistent, for people to engage. For many trans people they can be quite guarded, so also giving vulnerability to receive vulnerability often works.'

For Liane Hambly, authenticity and vulnerability can also be key when working with clients who are LGBTQIA+, as can understanding the shame that can carry, particularly in certain cultures. 'Clients, particularly younger ones, and from certain cultures, need to know it's a safe environment.' This doesn't mean going in too hard, as both Lee and Liane talked about going at the client's own pace and deciding what you share of your own personal circumstances. Liane also made other suggestions of how to support clients:

- Transitions – could be going through multiple at the same time (everything from gender to education) – tread carefully and go at their pace.

- Sharing your pronouns, even if you're not worried about sharing your own, can show you understand this matters to others, and in doing so create a safe space.

- Map their circle of resources and support, or access your own networks on their behalf, if they need, for example, mentors.

- Look at an employer's values and mission statement, and ask direct inclusivity questions at interview – see how they react.

- Be ready to get things wrong. As Liane puts it, 'that individual in front of you is still going to be very different, and what language they prefer, how they want to work might be different from what the theory says'.

- Making it better for one group is making it better for everyone. There are frameworks for things like career management and transition management, but think about which ones are best to use in each scenario. It's about that individual in front of you.

- Remember if you are trying to be someone you're not in order to be accepted, where you never feel you fit and you feel 'other', it can seriously affect your confidence and mental health. Think of ways you can help that client fit, from mapping the tribe they do have around them, to hanging up a rainbow flag as a show of support.

As a profession, we also need to get our own house in order. We are certainly not a diverse profession, and we need that diversity to enrich both the profession and provide better representation to support all our clients better. In the meantime, we can also educate ourselves, recognise our own biases and challenge systemic oppression in ourselves, others, and society. Social justice goes hand in hand with career work.

Summary

As if simply being a woman wasn't hard enough, there are additional barriers to and in the workplace, which many women have to navigate. But with the help of CDPs, navigating these things can become easier. Whether it's crafting their message to successfully ask for reasonable adjustments or learning how to thrive in a racially different environment, there are many ways CDPs can make a difference to their clients. This is particularly important when so many potential barriers can be minimised or removed altogether with the right support. CDPs can also be on hand to help clients work through some of these challenges, in a psychologically safe environment, where a sense of belonging, a key ingredient in inclusivity, can be fostered.

Tools

Here are some tools which you can use with your female clients, to help them understand you are a safe space, where they can be their true selves and not feel 'other', helping them to understand what they truly want out of life, how to go out and get it, and thrive at work.

General coaching questions relating to this topic

- What does success look like to you?
- What gives you the greatest sense of satisfaction in your life?
- Who do you feel most comfortable with and why?
- What strengths have you developed by navigating your unique challenges? How can those support you in the workplace?
- How will you benefit from this <insert the option they've discussed> type of work?

Inclusivity audit

This isn't a tool to use *with* clients, but one to use *for* them, helping you reflect on your own practice more broadly, not just session by session.

Ask yourself:

Language – Are you regularly using inclusive, accurate, and clear language?

- Instead of asking for 'preferred pronouns' (suggesting they are optional), state your own and invite theirs.
- Avoid phrases like 'I don't see colour' which erases racial identity – try 'I value diversity' instead.

- Use neutral, non-ableist terms (e.g., 'wheelchair user' not 'wheelchair-bound', and 'has', not 'suffers from').
- Avoid confusing metaphors or idioms, which can be unclear to neurodivergent clients. Full transparency – I struggle with this one! It's something I have to review regularly.
- If you're not sure what language you should be using, organisations like Stonewall and Disability Rights UK both have guides to promote non-discriminatory, inclusive communication.

Assumptions – What assumptions might you be making?

- Can you honestly say you're not making gender-based assumptions from someone's name or how they look?
- Don't assume a client's partner's gender or marital status.
- Remember not all disabilities can be seen, and tread carefully – you may think a client is neurodivergent but we're not medical professionals, and even if you're correct, they may not be aware or wish to share.

Environment – Is your setting accessible and comfortable?

- Is it wheelchair accessible, sensory-friendly, and safe for everyone? Even if you're working in education, no doubt in a cupboard for an office; this is where we need to advocate on behalf of our clients.
- Can you offer digital appointments (for those who can't leave the house), captions or alternative formats?
- Are your careers events inclusive and representative, with positive role models that can stop clients feeling 'other'?

Safety – What signals show you're a safe person to talk to?

- Do you display a Pride (rainbow) flag or poster, or wear a 'you're safe with me' badge or T-shirt?
- Don't assume people know you're inclusive; you need to show it.

Knowledge – Are you up to date on inclusive practice?

- Don't forget the *advice* bit of CEIAG – not just about supporting a client to learn about themselves, but also about giving advice, so include inclusivity as part of your CPD.
- Familiarise yourself with the law and research inclusive jobs boards (e.g., EmployAbility, BYP Network, myGwork).

You can explore these questions through self-reflection, peer discussion, or using a model like Gibbs' Reflective Cycle or the Wheel of Anything to guide your audit.

Identity mapping

If a client has spent much of their life feeling 'othered', exploring and re-evaluating their identity can be a powerful starting point.

You might explain: identity is like baking a cake; many ingredients make up the whole. Together, brainstorm aspects like gender, age, race, socio-economic background, education, relationships, sexuality, spirituality, and so on.

Ask the client to reflect on each area, noting what feels important. They might write 'Muslim' under spirituality or talk about how their age impacts their job search. Don't pressure; you'll know when to gently nudge or hold back. This can be sensitive.

To go deeper, use coaching questions like:

- Which parts of your identity feel empowering? Which feel vulnerable?
- How have these shaped your education, work, or relationships?
- How do these identities interact?
- What parts of your identity would you like to embrace more?
- What (or who) would help you bring your full self to work?

You can do this as a conversation, or with a worksheet showing identity categories in circles. Avoid boxes, as they subliminally suggest we're putting the client in one; we're not. For a more hands-on approach, use movable cut-out circles to layer identities almost like a Venn diagram, showing how they connect and overlap.

Challenge

If we're going to cheerlead our clients and encourage them to live to their full potential, there are lots of ways we can do that. One way is to challenge any preconceived ideas they may have or have been told. Kate Nash, in her own brilliant book *Positively Purple*, references the moment her mum talked about her getting 'a nice little job'. Using something like the GROW coaching model could help clients to assess all the options they do have, without limitations. I've used this model with clients many times, and the 'O' (Options) part of the model requires the most trust for your client to have in you. They need to put disbelief and barriers to one side and focus on what options there *could* be for them before then looking at how to make that happen.

The inclusion iceberg

As you've seen already, I LOVE an iceberg. The basic premise of an iceberg is that there is often a bit of iceberg that sits above the waterline that can be seen, and a whole load more underneath it that can't. It makes a brilliant metaphor for all sorts of things, and I'll be honest, is therefore often used in many of the training courses I run. And it's one that can definitely be used to work on the topic of identity and of drawing out the internalisation we've described in this chapter.

Using this as a metaphor, or drawing it on a piece of paper, ask what sits below and above that waterline. Questions like:

- Which parts of your identity are most visible to others?
- Which parts are invisible but strongly impact your life or work?
- Where have you experienced inclusion or exclusion?

SECTION 2
Understanding and celebrating wonderful you

Chapter 4
The (non)parent trap

Trigger warning: This chapter contains references to fertility issues and miscarriage. If you are affected by any of these topics, I hope you will find some solace through reading that you are not alone, but feel free to skip this chapter if needed.

The predictable conversation

It should have been a joyous occasion. One of my oldest friends was getting married. Unfortunately, that meant bumping into some people I'd not seen in years. And the questions started. What work do you do, are you married, and the old chestnut, do you have children? My story is not one of loss, so I don't mind that question, I really don't. What I do have a problem with is when I say that no, my partner and I have decided not to have children, the following was always inevitable.

> *Oh you don't want them, yet?*
> *What do you mean, you don't want them ever?*
> *Well why? Why, tell me why you've decided that?*
> *Oh it's just because your partner doesn't want them (an assumption on their part, not an actual fact).*
> *Oh well you'll regret it.*
> *So, tell me, why?*

The conversation would go on and on. Not for the first time or the last. The promotion of motherhood and the belief that it is the only option anyone wants or can have (pronatalism) is also common in the workplace. Well-intentioned 'women's groups' can become focused on motherhood issues, International Women's Day often emphasises supporting mothers to manage 'the juggle', and inclusivity intranet pages may focus on supporting parents, offering nothing for non-parents, all of which only increases this exclusion.

Likewise, policies and benefits packages tend to focus on parental support. Rightly so, parents do need support, but so do other women. Sam Walsh founded The Non-Mum network, a Facebook group, in 2017 in response to the loneliness and ostracisation she felt about being a woman without children. The 6,000 members who joined her showed she was not alone in this feeling. More women are now speaking out about the choices they've made, or that life has made for them. This 'one size fits all approach' to what women *should* or *must* do (i.e., have children) is no longer acceptable. As with so many of the challenges women face, however, there is still a long way to go. As Lucy Marie Hornsby points out, 'We need to stop assuming women are going to get to a certain age, and have children. In the pandemic everyone just assumed I was homeschooling.'

It is also important to remember that all women in the workplace, and therefore your clients, can't simply be put into two categories: mums and non-mums. The reality is far more, including:

- Parents of biological children;
- Parents of foster or adopted children;
- CFBC (Child Free By Choice);
- CNBC (Childless Not By Choice) and still trying to get pregnant or those who have stopped trying;
- CFBC/CNBC and now have stepchildren;
- Non-parents by circumstance;
- Grieving parents;
- Women suffering miscarriages or struggling with IVF;
- Adoptive parents or almost-parents who have had an adoptive process fall through;
- Solo parents;
- Step-parents through divorce or bereavement;
- Those who are as yet undecided.

Understanding what each one's needs are is critical to a successful relationship with your client or colleague.

The work-life conundrum

But why do you need to support your clients with this, if it's work you're focused on? Well, never have the worlds of work-life and home-life been more greatly merged as employers still try to manage flexible and hybrid working, and employees require a better work-life balance and greater wellbeing. This work-life balance goes beyond time management; it's about how much of your true self you want and need to bring to work, and how that impacts your career. It can impact in practical ways and emotional ones too. If you're constantly questioned about your life choices, it does nothing to help your confidence in how you live that life.

This particularly affects women, who have traditionally been seen as primary caregivers and, until relatively recently, were often excluded from financial independence like holding their own bank accounts or mortgages; factors that contributed to them being viewed less as career-focused individuals. But times have changed, with many women choosing to have children and work, or not have children, or have to juggle IVF alongside their career, or deal with child loss while still working, to name just a few challenges. So for them, never has the juggle of work and personal life become so blended. For HR and employers, that means creating environments where women can balance the two, and for careers professionals, it's about understanding that talking to a woman, or girl, about her career is going to involve so many other aspects of her life.

When I spoke to Emily Monsell-Holden, a brand specialist and TEDx speaker about her own fertility journey from IVF to acceptance of a life without children, she felt that 'it's an employer's responsibility to create a path where *all* women can fit in and have a safe space'. So if it's important that all employers, and CDPs, demonstrate they hold space for *all* women, how do they show that?

- Psychological safety where vulnerability is not just allowed, but encouraged.
- Clear contracting is essential, where trust can be built and an understanding of boundaries developed.
- Remember that at some point every woman is going to come across this 'decision' about children, whether it's willingly or not. And this will have some kind of bearing on her work-life.
- Fair approaches – many of the female clients I work with explain that as they don't have children, they're automatically expected to cover in the school holidays and are also made to feel an inconvenience when they then take time off later. As Emily puts it, 'I totally recognise that it is extremely hard to be a mother in the workplace and they should be supported as much as possible. When they're not, the people who don't have children have to pick up the slack. Seemingly small things like this are quite problematic.'

- Education – many of the challenges non-parents face in the workplace are often down to unwitting prejudice, so supporting our clients to educate their employers and encourage them to do more research themselves is key.
- There's a strong business case for supporting all employees. As careers professionals, it's vital to help clients identify inclusive workplaces, ask the right questions during recruitment, and, when needed, seek legal advice once in role.
- Meet clients where they are. A woman without children might not be overly career ambitious, just as a woman with a whole troop of children might have big ambitious plans for her career. Likewise, Lucy Marie suggests we 'need to be more honest about the impact of parenting options on a woman's career. My career development is different, as I don't have children; I don't have to worry about income in the same way, I can be flexible with what I do, and I've chosen that.'

The impact on careers

Prejudice does also work both ways. As well as making women without children feel 'other', all women can be discriminated against over pregnancy fears. While pregnancy may be a protected characteristic in the workplace, many conversations happen behind closed doors. I've been managed by an HR Director who questioned my hiring decision, fearing the woman with a toddler would likely go on maternity leave again soon. She was the right candidate for the job, so I hired her. Elizabeth Willetts, a recruitment specialist and founder of a flexible working recruitment business, has had many similar conversations, including an employer debating whether to hire a 40- or 30-year-old. 'They went with the 40-year-old, because they were worried the woman in her 30s would get pregnant.'

This kind of discrimination is often based on gendered assumptions that aren't even accurate. For example, in 2021, around 69.1% of women without dependent children were in the UK workforce (ONS, 2021), and conception rates among women in their 40s have continued to rise (ONS, 2023). So, by making assumptions, employers risk rejecting great candidates, whether it's someone who never plans to have children or someone older who may still choose to become a parent.

And as for those who do choose to have children, they may take a short maternity leave break, or much longer, potentially spending years out of the workforce while they look after their children.

CDPs can help women in this situation in a variety of ways, including:

- Advise clients to make use of KIT (Keep in Touch days) and also more casual catch-ups, like having a coffee with old colleagues. This can form part of a client's plan for their return, set before they leave, and include other elements such as how much they want to be kept in the loop while they're off.

- Support clients with ways to keep upskilling – from listening to podcasts, to watching YouTube videos or buying cheap courses on places like Udemy can all help, and as Elizabeth points out will help 'keep a toe in and build your confidence'.

- For many women, having a baby creates a whole identity shift, and going back to work after this can be challenging. CDPs can help by using the tools in the book to help clients to realign with who they are: their purpose, their values, their strengths and skills in this 'new' version of them. Encourage them to dig out old performance reviews and other feedback to remind them of who they were and if that still feels like a good fit.

- For those who have been off for longer periods, doing additional work on how the workplace has changed, how their skills now fit and how they sell this new version of themselves will also be key. Also, coach them through where any lack of confidence may be coming from, for example, is it not feeling up to date and relevant or competent, and then help them plan how to address that.

- CDPs and HR can also support by encouraging employers to provide the right kind of support for female returners. Elizabeth agrees, saying the success of this is down to how well they are onboarded. 'When I went back after maternity, I felt like a new starter; everyone had moved on and I couldn't even remember my password. My identity had shifted and my employer was acting like it was Monday and I'd only been off since Friday.' Encouraging employers to provide, and our clients to look out for, companies who will support with even just a few weeks of additional support could make all the difference.

- Encourage clients to 'fill their cup'. Reflect with them on what makes them happy in their personal life, putting them in a good headspace to thrive at work and even generate career ideas. It's key during this time to do things that uplift you, whether that's exercise, eating, cooking, or spending time with people who lift you up, all this self-care can give you a confidence boost. This could be relevant for both women already with a professional background and when working with young people. Using Holland's RIASEC Model (see Tools), you can evaluate their interests, passions, hobbies, and how these could generate careers ideas. Focus on what they are interested in, not on gender-based stereotype assumptions.

Female returners

Whether it's been a short maternity break or longer, many women struggle when moving back into the workplace. HR training providers DPG found the same, with 88% of mothers experiencing problems returning to work after maternity leave (FE News, 2018). Many experience refusals for part-time work or are allowed on a lower salary, and new employers focus on the career break rather than the much higher percentage of time they've spent in work, doing great things.

But employers who focus on this are missing a trick. Elizabeth suggests that 'if you treat women well, you're going to get very loyal employees and get to retain all their skills and knowledge in your business.' Ayo Sobo-Keane adds, 'I've worked a four-day week since my son was born, and it's a two-way street. Work is flexible with me, so I'm flexible with them.'

CDPs can support women by helping them position career breaks as strengths, build assertiveness to advocate for themselves, and understand that rejections may stem from bias. They can also guide women in developing a personal brand that highlights both professional and parenting skills.

Flexibility for all

Flexible work environments can be key to helping women thrive professionally, and it's something CDPs can support their clients to review, seek, and advocate for, whatever their reasons for asking. As of 6 April 2024, under the Employment Relations (Flexible Working) Act 2023, any employee in the UK can request flexible working from their very first day in a role and it's no longer limited to parents or those with caring responsibilities. Employers aren't required to agree, but they must consult with the employee, respond within two months, and clearly explain their business reasons for refusal, rather than simply rejecting the request if it's not childcare related.

As well as requesting flexible work for a current role, for some women, they'll be looking for a new role which is flexible from the start. Studies show women are less likely to apply for a role and ask about flexible working arrangements if it is not explicitly stated on the ad. Elizabeth says this is a common scenario as 'only 3% of jobs are advertised as part-time. So chances are you're going to have to apply for a role that doesn't mention flexibility, and negotiate that. Often I find employers are open to it, they've just not thought to mention it.' And often they are open to it as they can see it helps to build diverse, profitable teams and can improve, not reduce, things like productivity. As Elizabeth points out, her compressed hours increase her productivity: 'I don't have time to procrastinate, I just get the work done before the school run.'

Likewise, for those without children, flexibility can be important too, but traditionally hasn't always been accepted. As was Emily's experience, who feels the boundaries of flexibility need to be expanded; 'it is so often talked about regarding parenting or caring responsibilities. If you're a woman without children applying for flexibility, it's confusing for everyone. When I wanted to go down to four days a week, my manager was supportive but the employer was against it, they wouldn't sign it off as they were worried that then everyone would want it. It's not flexible working if it only applies to parents of young children, that is parental working hours.' Ayo feels, however, that employers who take this approach are missing a trick. 'If offering flexibility works for one group of women, why wouldn't it work for another?'

Flexibility can also be offered in more specific scenarios, where creating a safe, respectful space, such as giving employees the option to work from home during triggering events, like baby showers, can make a big difference. Ayo agrees, sharing her own journey with IVF and felt that 'situations where you would find it hard to be at work, like people bringing in babies, I don't feel is for your employer to shield you from that. But if you wanted to have a day at home, I do feel you should be able to ask.' Emily also suggests that recognising other celebrations beyond 'the hetro-normative pipeline that could be celebrated too, beyond engagement, marriage and babies' would produce a more inclusive environment.

CDPs can help here by:

- Supporting their client in getting really clear on what they want and why, before asking for flexibility.

- Crafting their message to include a clear business case which is more difficult to say 'no' to.
- As part of that message, identifying any potential hurdles and addressing them head on, showing solutions or workarounds.
- Support clients to bring out their assertive champion; they're not being bolshy, they're asking for what they legally can. Base this request around business case data of why it's good for the business as much as the employee, and they'll feel better about selling their case.
- Also support clients with the concept that it's OK if you don't have children and only want to work part-time, that's your choice. Lucy Marie highlights, 'There is so much pressure on women to be a certain way. Just because you don't have children doesn't mean you have to go on luxurious holidays, or be working all the time, or have a side hustle. If you want to work part-time and potter about in your garden and rest, that's OK.'

Line managers

Another area CDPs can help their clients is identifying the inclusive cultures and managerial support they need to thrive, and then research those. It's something I encourage all my clients to think about before worrying about job titles or salary. Without the right environment, a flower can't grow. And for some women, this is even more important.

Emily explains that during her fertility struggles, line manager support was crucial. 'I had a very supportive manager who understood my need for flexibility and space. I was fortunate that I had that; otherwise, it would have been impossible.' Likewise, for women with children, having an understanding line manager can help shape their career. From flexibility around school pick-ups to kindness after a sleepless night, it can help support women who would otherwise be fearful of speaking out.

Policies and procedures

Company policies can be powerful tools for women seeking support at work. These might include legal entitlements like the Flexible Working Bill (Gov, 2023) and Maternity support, or company-specific policies around IVF, menopause, or neonatal bereavement. They should protect both employees and the business while being inclusive of all staff.

However, a ResumeLab study found 74% of respondents believed parents were treated better than non-parents, and 87% felt parents had more benefits. Childless workers reported being denied leave, given heavier workloads, or expected to cover unsociable shifts to accommodate parents. While this data is from the US, similar issues exist in the UK. Flexibility for parents is valuable, but true inclusivity means offering the same consideration to others, whether for fertility treatment, menopause symptoms, or simply wanting time off during school holidays even without childcare requirements.

HR may lead on policies, but fairness is everyone's responsibility. Companies should ask:

- Does our bereavement policy cover miscarriage?
- Does our IVF policy also support unsuccessful cycles, for example, offering mental health support?
- Can flexibility be offered in other circumstances, even on a temporary basis, for example, to support a female employee who wants to do an IVF injection at home or the mother dealing with a temporary childcare issue?

By considering the needs of all employees, organisations build psychological safety, allowing people to feel supported and thrive. CDPs can help clients identify inclusive cultures and ask the right questions about policies during recruitment.

Ayo felt that while company policies are important, 'often it doesn't have to be official, it's just about human kindness'. A company might not have a relevant policy, but a line manager making their own decision to empower their employee is all that is needed. As Elizabeth shared, 'When I was going through IVF, my company didn't have an official policy but my manager was kind and I was able to pop to appointments or work from home after transfer days. I was lucky, as many women end up dropping out of work if they don't get this support but my advice to them, is don't! You'll want the maternity pay if you do get pregnant, and also for me, work gave me an outlet, something else to focus on. I'd love to see more companies with official policies though, so you know where you stand.'

As CDPs, we also need to show empathy. Clients may be dealing with fertility struggles, sleep deprivation from parenting, or other personal challenges.

Meeting them where they are and offering flexible support is key to helping them move forward.

Summary

Women in the workplace have diverse personal circumstances, whether they have children or not, which can significantly impact their experience at work. From offering flexible working to using inclusive language in policies and simply showing empathy, there's much for HR and businesses to consider. As career professionals and HR partners, we can support women by helping them identify what they need, craft their message in a way that resonates with employers, and build their confidence to speak up. Creating a psychologically safe environment where honest, often difficult conversations are welcomed is key to fostering belonging and helping women thrive.

As Emily puts it, 'The things that women want and need; the flexibility, the respect, the tools to do their job, I don't know anybody, man or woman, that doesn't want that for themselves.' Indeed, making it better for women is making it better for everyone, much like making the workplace better for mums is making it better for non-mums, and vice versa. Or as I like to put it: it's the workplace that needs fixing, not the women.

Tools

Here are some tools you can use with your female clients, to help them grow confidence in their life and career choices, and craft their message to employers.

General coaching questions relating to this topic

- What must you have in your life to make you feel complete, fulfilled, and happy?
- What does success look like to you?
- Decision-making. If you say yes to this, what are you saying no to (and vice versa)?
- What motivates you in life and at work?
- What lifestyle do you want?

Jigsaw career

'Kintsugi' is the Japanese art of taking something broken, often pottery, and sticking it back together, to make something more beautiful. Rather than trying to disguise the cracks, they are enhanced with things like gold, so the overall item becomes even more beautiful than before. Sometimes for our clients, they may need a bit of help in understanding their life can be like that, especially if they have gone through trauma such as fertility treatments, or even happy events like childbirth. Who even are they anymore?

Using either actual jigsaw pieces or pieces drawn out on paper, ask the client to take each piece in turn. Explain that each jigsaw piece represents a particular part of them. Taking one piece at a time, ask them to assign a part of them to that piece. For example, they could be 'great at working with others' or 'feel very spiritual'. It could be anything from their values, their skills, or things they have been through or decisions they've made; all make up who they are. This activity is about getting the client comfortable and confident with who they are and how the pieces of the puzzle that have made up their life so far make them the brilliant person they are. This is really about asking them to identify, 'what makes you, you?' This links to their identity, which, as Elizabeth points out, 'can shift'. Using a Wheel of Life could be another way to do this.

Find your tribe

As this chapter has shown, whatever your personal circumstances, not seeing others 'like you' can feel isolating. One way to boost confidence is to identify who's already in your corner, or who could be. This isn't just about workplace connections; it's about your whole support network.

Encourage clients to take an A3 sheet and place a photo or drawing of themselves at the centre, then build out a mind map of their network, like LinkedIn on paper. Who are their current connections? Who could they be introduced to through those people? Then reflect: who among this network might truly understand me? Who feels like a safe person to talk to?

Building strong, authentic connections creates a personal 'tribe' and sense of belonging, and with that, confidence naturally grows.

Another way to further develop a client's sense of belonging is to also offer group coaching. Among the many benefits, Bandura (1977) suggested four key ways for an individual to increase their career self-efficacy. Two of those were vicarious experiences and affirming feedback; both of which can be developed more strongly through group coaching.

Circle of Control/Influence

People don't leave bad jobs; they leave bad managers. We've all heard that, right? Well, it's kind of true. It's certainly often the daily frustrations that grind us down, frustrate us, and knock our confidence as we're left feeling helpless and as if whatever we do makes no difference. This can also be true when we're job hunting and getting nowhere or potentially making life decisions such as trying for a baby.

In these circumstances, it can be helpful to talk through with a client what is in their Circle of Control (they have full 'power' over), Circle of Influence (they can impact it but it's also down to external factors), and what is completely out of their control. Mapping it in this way can help realign thinking and also action plans of next steps, focusing on the things the client can change.

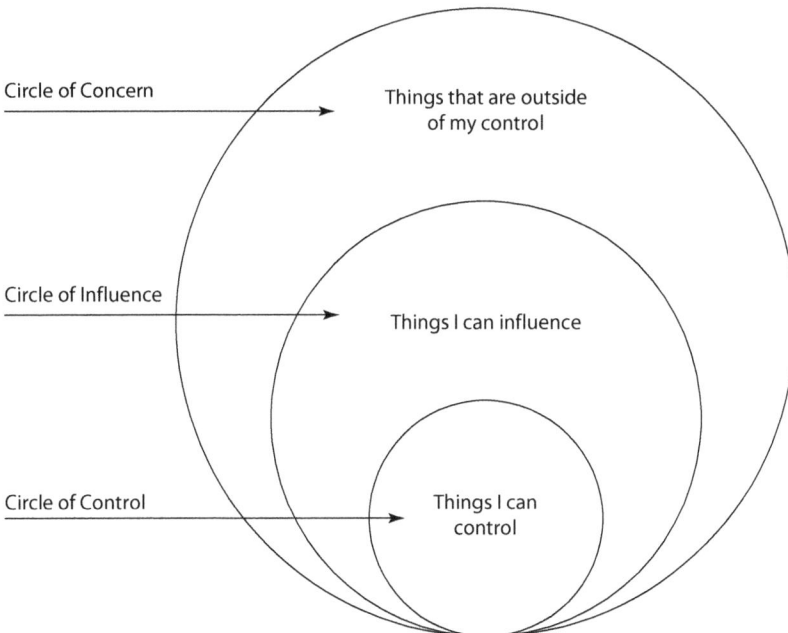

Circle of Concern — Things that are outside of my control

Circle of Influence — Things I can influence

Circle of Control — Things I can control

Holland's RIASEC model

Holland identified six personality types, each associated with particular interests, values, and preferred work environments (see table). Ask your client to reflect on their favourite hobbies and activities and then discuss which of those might fit in any particular category. From this, you can then explore with them career ideas which may align with the different personality types.

	Realistic – enjoys physical, hands-on activities	Investigative – curious about science and problem-solving	Artistic – creative and expressive	Social – likes helping others and working in groups	Enterprising – motivated by leadership and persuasion	Conventional – prefers structure and organisation
Do you have any hobbies, activities, or interests which might fit in this category?						

This table is available as part of the online resources that accompany this book. To access, scan the QR code or visit the web address at the start of this book.

What is your why?

Being assertive is regularly frowned upon for women. If we are assertive, we're often dismissed as pushy or bolshy, but we need to help clients change this rhetoric. Elizabeth explains that she often asks the question: 'If you're not having this conversation, what will your life be like?' If you've not asked for a flexible working pattern, will you be rushing to the school gates, missing nativities, always relying on others for childcare or missing important work deadlines?

It's a good question. So is one of my favourite coaching questions: 'If you're saying yes to this, what are you saying no to?' And vice versa.

A helpful exercise is to ask clients to draw a vertical line down a sheet of paper, labelling one side 'Yes' and the other 'No'. Then, have them list everything they currently do, from specific tasks like attending meetings to everyday habits like picking up after others.

Next, explore the trade-offs. For example, saying *yes* to doing others' laundry might mean saying *no* to watching *Corrie* or *Love Is Blind*. Or saying *yes* to a meeting might mean *no* to being overlooked for promotions, because they're showing up and being visible.

Emphasise that *no* isn't always negative; it often makes space for a more meaningful *yes*. Finally, ask, 'Are there any items you'd like to move to the other column? And why?' When clients understand their *why*, it becomes easier to make and stand by intentional choices.

Journaling activity

Some clients may carry a lot of internal 'noise' around the topic of parental status, often deeply personal and not something they wish to share openly. Starting a session with some journaling can help them enter a reflective, focused state. I've suggested prompt questions around the theme of success, as clients may need support in defining, or redefining, what success truly means to them. Women are often handed a narrow definition of success, particularly around how they 'should' be mothers, but real progress comes when they define success on their own terms. Only when they feel clear and confident in that definition can they effectively communicate it to others.

Be clear that they don't need to share what they've written, unless they want to.

Begin by asking them to do some wild writing – five minutes of just jotting down all the things that come to mind, with no filter.

Then give them about one minute or so for each of the following questions (or design your own):

- What does success look like to you?
- What might help you with this? What might hinder?
- Who might be able to help you achieve this?
- What would you say to your younger self about the journey they are on?

You could invite them to share their thoughts, or even a more gentle 'was there anything about what you've written that surprised you?' But remind them to only share what/if they wish.

Chapter 5
The Imposter
Monster and other
scary tales

One of my first jobs after university was working on a leadership development programme for teachers. I coordinated events and attended as a participant evaluator. At the end of one course, we had a feedback session. Each participant had to write a 'plus' and 'minus' at the top of their flip chart pad. The group gave feedback on the individual and they then assigned that to whichever column they felt appropriate. We were encouraged to be supportive, yet thorough and constructive in our feedback and not hold back. All suitably terrified, we began the session.

'You're thoughtful,' said one delegate to the first volunteer.

They headed straight to the 'minus' column and wrote, 'Awful'.

A brief pause. A collective gasp! Then hurried explanations that the volunteer had misheard. They were positively thoughtful and far from awful.

Can you imagine? Being that person and thinking the first piece of feedback was that you're awful! The thing is, you probably can. Because it got me thinking, why are we so quick to think the worst of ourselves, and that others will view us that way too? As humans, we are complex; there are many reasons we might feel this way. From evolution, where a mind focused on potential threats helped us to stay alive, to the more modern world of comparing ourselves to others. It's the illness I call 'comparitonitus'. But as we stare at our phones at that impossibly youthful and slim celebrity (whose using a filter on her phone too 'techy' for us to even understand), or watch videos of our friends having a blast while we're doing the cleaning, it can really mess with our minds. It seems everyone has it together, apart from us. And that's a very quick path to letting in what I call the 'Imposter Monster'. Addressing it this way can be helpful with clients; detaching 'self' from the 'monster' can help to distinguish fact from fiction. Lee Gilbert also agrees, saying, 'Think of the imposter as an entity, not part of yourself. It may sit alongside you, but you choose to listen or shut that out.'

The 'imposter' among us

So what do we mean when we talk about this concept of feeling like an imposter? It can be explained as the persistent belief that your success is undeserved or that you're a 'fraud' despite evidence of competence. This negativity bias and inner critic lead people to fixate on their perceived shortcomings while dismissing or minimising their achievements. They fear they are an imposter and it is only a matter of time before everyone finds out. Gemma Brown, a coach, goes on to explain that it is about internal vs external. 'It's about internalising this fraudulent feeling, a sense that you don't belong, regardless of your external success. In this mindset we fail to recognise the role we play in our own success.'

The topic of 'imposter' is often described as imposter syndrome, having come into everyday parlance following a study conducted by psychologists Pauline Rose Clance and Suzanne Ament Imes in 1978 and their paper, titled *The Impostor Phenomenon in High Achieving Women: Dynamics and Therapeutic Intervention*. In this research, they identified a pattern where high-achieving women, despite evident success, internalised feelings of intellectual phoniness and feared being exposed as frauds (Clance & Imes, 1978). Originally known as imposter phenomenon, this became known as imposter syndrome. At the time, Clance and Imes believed the phenomenon was more prevalent among women due to societal and familial pressures. However, subsequent research has shown that imposter feelings affect people of all genders.

So is it just a 'woman's problem' or not?

The simple answer: no. It can, and does, affect many people, but certain groups such as women report higher challenges. How it is described is also different. Farrah Morgan, a grad coach, agrees, explaining that often it's simply about the language used. She highlights that her female clients tend to focus more on their 'own "self-condition" so they use "imposter syndrome" a lot, whereas I don't tend to hear male clients say that, but they're all talking about the same thing'. Gemma also found that her male coaching clients do have these feelings but use different language; they 'want to perform better, achieve a set goal, but through coaching they realise it's imposter feelings holding them back'. Society has told them to be confident and not talk about feelings, whereas for women it's quite the opposite. Gemma suggests how this can play into imposter feelings; when asked to speak up at work, women can struggle because until this point, 'lots of clients I work with have that "good girl" script – be quiet, be good, be small, be thankful for where you are'.

As CDPs, we can support women to use their voice, and Mo (Mousumi) Kanjilal highlights the need for this. 'Women sometimes feel they have to say they experience imposter syndrome, as it sounds arrogant to not. But not every woman feels that; sometimes we are confident, we just need to be heard.' Likewise, if a woman is struggling in the workplace, it's also important to not just assume that's down to imposter feelings. Is it that, or is it culturally they're being excluded, is it their own hormones playing tricks on their mind, or something else? Women need to be detectives, and CDPs can support them with this.

It's also important to consider the intersectionality here, including for those from minorities experiencing greater imposter syndrome, alongside the challenges of fewer women in leadership, meaning women are more likely to be managed by men, who may take different approaches. Neither may be right or wrong, but they can internalise the assumption that they are wrong. And CDPs can help them draw this belief out and address it.

It's also important that imposter thoughts and feelings are not described as a syndrome, as it's not an illness. And because it's not, there are ways we can address them – including during careers sessions through:

1. Education – what it means, how it manifests, understanding you're not alone.

2. Identifying – is it actually imposter thoughts and feelings or are you actually being excluded? These feelings are particularly common when:

   ● You're being visible/feeling exposed, for example, applying for a new job, speaking in a meeting, or presenting;

   ● When you're doing something new;

   ● When you're in the minority.

3. Not being afraid to share – if we hold onto the feelings alone, it only gives them room to breathe and magnifies them.

These fears are hard to break, often tied to fear of failure and perfectionism. As CDPs, we can help especially those early in their careers, since many employers report younger workers hesitate to try due to fear of failing. Early on, fear is natural, but mistakes fuel learning. Encouraging a growth mindset helps clients build resilience and better manage their careers.

The impact on careers

However, achieving this can be challenging, and without it, clients may struggle to move forward in their careers. This can result in a sense of career paralysis. In their study, *When People Don't Realize Their Career Desires: Toward a Theory of Career Inaction*, Verbruggen and De Vos (2020) suggest why people often do not follow through on their career aspirations, as they go through:

- Awareness Phase: Individuals recognise a desire for change in their career.
- Inaction Phase: Despite the desire for change, individuals fail to take sufficient action over a period of time.
- Recall Phase: Individuals look back and regret not having taken action.

They suggest the inaction phase might be down to a number of factors including:

- Difficulties in making decisions;
- Anxiety about potential outcomes;
- Payoff for staying vs long-term goals;
- Cognitive overload;
- Social norms;
- Fear of letting people down.

This can be particularly challenging for women, who may experience many of these barriers. Together, these factors can make taking career action feel overwhelming. Using the following tools, addressing imposter challenges may be the crucial first step in helping a client move forward in their career.

Contracting

If you have a client who is wrestling with their Imposter Monster, contracting now becomes more important than ever. Be sure to discuss the idea of you challenging them as a supportive tool, and not because you think they're wrong. After all, if they're questioning themselves already, you questioning too could be problematic. Likewise, using the tool of silence is still very useful, but be mindful it doesn't allow for your client to go down an 'imposter rabbit hole' with their thoughts; this is where comfortable challenge becomes all important and getting the right balance between speaking and listening.

How to beat the Imposter Monster?

As with all aspects of careers work, there's no 'one size fits all' approach. It starts with understanding your client. How do imposter feelings show up for them? What's driving it – a specific event, their background, or a mix of things? Avoid making assumptions.

When I first set up my business and nervously headed off to a full day of school appointments, my partner was baffled. To him, this was the easy bit, something I'd done for years. But for me, everything felt different: a new environment, new students, and for the first time, I was representing *myself* and my company brand. That brought a pressure I hadn't felt before. It was a reminder not to make assumptions and how easy it is to miss what's really going on beneath the surface. The same is true with our clients. We need to meet them where they are, not where we assume they'll be.

Having said that, there are some 'rules' which will likely be helpful when working with most clients, including:

- First step – renaming these imposter thoughts and feelings or 'monster' to refer to them as self-limiting beliefs. The 'monster' is the incorrect thoughts/feelings, but we're the ones allowing it in and putting limitations on ourselves. We can change our mindset.

- A way to do this is to establish fraud from fact, for example, reviewing your skills, strengths, qualifications, and even gathering feedback from others.

- All too often we focus on 'fixing' our weaknesses; make sure your clients take regular moments to celebrate their strengths, their achievements, the things they're actually proud of (see the next chapter for more on this). Spend time here. Clients can be slow to start generating ideas if they're busy with their imposter, but start small and build up and make it a regular habit.

- Sometimes it's not about imposter feelings – it's about being afraid to say how great we are, and how confident we feel, because of what society says. Use the tools below to help your client break out of these chains and show the world how truly wonderful they are.

- If you're working with managers, encourage training around this topic. Often they'll say to employees that they don't need to have imposter issues or, as Gemma puts it, 'just have more confidence in yourself and then you'd be great'. This helps no one. Specific feedback on their strengths, as well as actionable steps to address blind spots, is far more useful.

Reframing

Another way to deal with the Imposter Monster is to reframe it. Gemma explained that she often invites her clients to 'think of the imposter voice as a protector; rather than shunning it, ask, "What is it trying to protect you from?"' As a CDP, encourage people to talk about it, bringing it out of the dark and normalise it. Your goal here is to get the client to bring their emotions to the surface, acknowledge them, and make sense of them. An acknowledged emotion has the opportunity to change. But note the importance of supporting the client to not judge themselves for having that emotion.

Encouraging clients to think of the role they played in positive outcomes can also be a good tool to not only squash the Imposter Monster but also understand why it is there in the first place. They may have a fear of speaking up in a meeting, having been ridiculed before. But if you can understand and reframe that, maybe it was someone who was threatened by their great ideas in the past, this could encourage them to speak up when in a more supportive culture, as their ideas are clearly great.

Testing

An alternative to reframing is to test the behaviour. Behaviour experiments are a psychological technique most closely associated with Cognitive Behavioural Therapy (CBT). They are experimental activities which can be used to test the accuracy of a client's beliefs or assumptions, through direct experience. This can be a good platform to externalise these traits, rather than internalise. As Gemma puts it, 'When we do this, we take those problematic attributes as us, we can't differentiate ourselves from them and that makes us think we can't change.' Testing them out, however, can change this mindset. Here, you ask a client to identify a belief, plan a safe way to test the belief, ask the client what they're expecting to happen, and then get them to test it out. After the event, reflect back with the client on what actually happened and what they can learn.

Challenge

As well as asking clients to reframe their thoughts, we too as CDPs can reframe how we ask our questions, to greater effect. For example, if a client tells us they are 'not good enough', a common statement among the world of Imposter Monsters, we could ask, 'In what ways are you not good enough?' But Gemma points out, a much better question could be 'What about you allows these imposter thoughts and feelings of being not good enough to intrude?' In doing so, it separates the individual client from these thoughts and allows them control over changing the narrative.

Job descriptions — watch the imposter fly

Have you seen that anti-bullying advert where a young child has a furry monster as his sidekick? Every time someone says something mean, the furry monster gobbles it up and gets bigger. I think of the Imposter Monster like that. And if there is one place it can have a feeding frenzy, it's during job hunting.

There is a common theory that women's Imposter Monsters are the greediest here. This is often linked to an internal study by Hewlett-Packard that found women will only apply for a role if they meet 100% of the criteria and for men it's just 60%. This data is hard to prove, and as CDPs we need to be careful not to feed into a narrative which makes women even less sure of themselves. Instead, we need to be client-centred as always, and find out what's holding that client back from applying for a particular role. Helping them assess, do they genuinely not meet the criteria, or is confidence holding them back.

However, research in the Harvard Business Review suggests women not applying for roles is less about confidence and more about following the rules. If they don't meet 100% of the criteria, they may feel they're wasting the recruiter's time or doing something wrong (Mohr, 2014). So it's not just about building self-belief; it's also about helping clients gain confidence in *playing the game* of job hunting and putting themselves forward.

Of more significance might be the actual wording used in adverts. A study by Technische Universität München found that women were less likely to apply to job ads containing masculine-coded words like 'determined' and 'assertive', while they responded more positively to communal terms such as 'dedicated', 'responsible', and 'conscientious' (Technische Universität München, 2022). Ruth Forster, as a recruiter in the manufacturing industry, struggles with this. 'I've talked about advertising roles before, we advertised for a Manufacturing Director and received 77 applications, not one single woman applied. I questioned myself and wondered if we hadn't used the "right" wording to attract male and female candidates, but the reality is, the wording related to the needs of the job, and this is a challenging job, if I change the wording would this impact the fit for the culture of the organisation? It's maybe not the advert that's the issue, it's the culture and demand of the industry.'

So how can CDPs help? Understanding and building strengths, knowing how these relate to other ways of describing the same words and unpacking what, for example, the word 'leader' truly means. You can also support by ensuring the language you use, or the resources you provide, from card activities to websites with job portfolios, can be explained. Distil words that might be barriers and link them to the strengths of the individual client.

There is also something around asking clients 'what does success look like to you?' and strategies to get there. Discussions around barriers and how they could overcome them, and talking about who they have in their tribe to help them overcome obstacles, are all great ways of building confidence. This helps create a clear resilience plan to weather the career storms, so they can positively move forward and not hold themselves back.

Journaling and imagery

One of the challenges with addressing imposter feelings is that they're based around an idea of failure, of not being 'good enough' and, as a result, a fear of being 'found out'. So asking a client or colleague to share these can be challenging. A great way to tackle this can be to try a journaling approach. Gemma also highlights there are many other benefits, including 'research studies show that it's about finding lightness, clarity, mood, improving sleep and confidence'. There are many other benefits, and one that is often spoken about is the feeling that it can be a great way to 'untangle the mind'.

This can be a useful tool to work with all clients and, as Gemma suggests, it can be helpful to offer as a tool if 'clients are talking about wellbeing, or boundaries or with women it's often about mental load and overwhelm, managing busyness and how to prioritise, journaling is a great tool for those things'. There are ways of supporting your clients to do this, including giving time for 'wild writing', a practice where they just write down anything that comes to mind, with no agenda, no filter, no judgement. This can be a really useful way to settle clients into a session if they've arrived with a busy mind, or straight from a meeting, and so on. It can give them a moment of calm to gather their thoughts and get rid of the distractions. You can also support clients more directly, giving journaling prompts on a particular topic or theme during a session, just as you would with coaching questions, but here you're not asking them to speak their thoughts, but write them down. And you can also give these questions as prompts between sessions.

Like journaling, there is also scope for other creative pursuits such as using imagery and/or artistic endeavours. I personally have a journal which is a mixture of writing, both wild writing and using journaling prompts (you could get these from anywhere, including books with coaching questions or even AI), and then also some artwork. I use the term loosely; there is no chance any of my pictures and collages will end up in the Tate, but that's not the point. It's a moment for me to take stock, to empty out the noise in my head, to take a moment to breathe and make sense of how I'm feeling. When you're suffering from imposter feelings in particular, as we've discussed, a key thing is to separate fact from fiction in your mind and this is a great way to do this.

It's important if you are doing this with a client that you don't force them to share what they've written, but invite them to share anything they feel comfortable with – this could be either specifics of what they've written or more general comments about what they're noticing, like 'wow there was a lot in my head today'. This can then be a platform for further coaching questions.

Of all the senses, sight and how our brains process images happens faster than other things, such as hearing someone speak or reading and understanding the written word. So using imagery in coaching can be a really effective tool. Coaching with collage is a tool I regularly use, and I find you can go to a deeper level with clients much more quickly.

Both these practices can help clients address the deeply personal issue of limiting beliefs and imposter thoughts and feelings, and can be a great way to ease into further conversation.

Summary

In this chapter we have looked at imposter thoughts and feelings, reframing them as a 'monster' separate from self, which we can overcome. There are a number of ways to help your clients achieve this, including:

- Learning what it is, how it manifests, and how common it is.
- Articulating strengths and other positives as a way of combating it.
- Identifying not everyone has it, and not all the time. Be a detective and find if there is another issue at play.
- Try reframing it or testing beliefs in controlled ways.
- Using tools like journaling and imagery to help clients tap into their inner feelings.

It's also important to note that it's not just women who suffer from imposter thoughts and feelings, and through careful contracting with a client, we can challenge untrue or unhelpful beliefs they hold about themselves. We can also support clients to move from inaction and understand they have the power to change the situation.

And to all the wonderful women out there, isn't it about time you started to do things with intent, rather than worry about potential consequences, stop apologising for who you are, and start smashing that glass ceiling?!

Tools

Here are some tools which you can use with your female clients, helping them grow in confidence, know their worth, and quieten that Imposter Monster.

Coaching questions

- What are you assuming about yourself that might be holding you back?
- When you have faced challenges in the past, how have you overcome them?

- What three things are you most proud of? What can you learn about these for moving forward?
- How can you be as kind and forgiving of yourself as you are to others?
- What does saying no mean you say yes to, and vice versa?
- What failures have you experienced and what did you learn from them? This is a powerful reframe and helpful if people are very negative and can't see anything to be proud of; they'll definitely be able to find 'failures'. Your role is to then help them reframe them as learning tools.

These can also be used as journaling prompts, or invite clients to draw pictures or pull out images, which represent their answers. Use these to further explore what is happening for them in this moment.

Post-it notes activity

Hi, I'm Caroline and I'm a stationery addict. My favourite careers tool? The Post-it note. Born from a failed glue experiment – an important message in itself about learning through failure – it is now something many of us rely on.

Ask your client to write down individual words they'd use to describe themselves or labels/words others have used. One word/phrase per post-it. Then stick them onto their chest and one by one ask:

- Is it helpful?
- Is it true?
- Can it be reframed?
- Sometimes asking where it came from is also useful intel, or when it started?

Then ask the client what they want to do – keep, reframe, or ditch. A simple tool which can have positive results on how that client truly feels about the ideas they are holding on to.

'What ifs' bingo

A lot of imposter feelings centre on 'what if' … 'what if I speak up and everyone laughs at me?', 'what if I can't do this?', 'what if everyone realises I can't?', and so on. This activity challenges how often those 'what ifs' become things that actually happen (or not).

Make up a bingo card (revision cards with a boxed grid drawn on are perfect), with some of the client's 'what ifs' thoughts written in. Tell them to take it away and every time one of those 'what ifs' happens, put a cross in the box (like bingo). Use it on an ongoing basis – either note when they don't get filled out, challenging how likely those 'what ifs' actually are, or discuss what happened if they did put a cross, and how they coped and what they can learn.

Be a detective

Ask your client to describe a situation when they felt energised.

- What was going on?
- Who was involved?
- What did you actually do? And what were the consequences?
- How did you feel afterwards? What thoughts were going round your head?

Now ask the client to describe a situation where they felt uncomfortable. Ask the bullet questions again.

What can your client learn from each of these experiences about what is happening for them right now? Are there patterns? For example, they might notice that their manager being around goes hand in hand with them feeling uncomfortable. Is this really an issue of imposter syndrome, or is it a case of the client not feeling supported?

The 5 Whys

This is a simple but powerful root-cause analysis technique used to explore the underlying reasons behind a problem by repeatedly asking 'why?' Usually, you ask this five times until the core issue is uncovered. This helps clients move beyond surface-level symptoms and gain deeper self-awareness by identifying the real drivers behind their thoughts, behaviours, or challenges. For example, if a client says they feel stuck in their career, the coach might ask, 'Why do you feel stuck?' and follow each response with another 'why?'-based question, gently guiding the client to reflect more deeply. This encourages critical thinking, uncovers limiting beliefs, and supports more meaningful goal-setting and personal growth. It's one of my personal favourite tools in its simplicity but power.

Chapter 6
What makes you, YOU?

It's funny what stays with you. Over 20 years ago, I went on a training course led by the brilliant coach Will Thomas. On the first day, he told us he wouldn't call us back from breaks; he'd just play a song to signify it was time to come back. Simple idea, but it worked.

The song was 'Superstar' by Jamelia. To this day, whenever I hear it, I think, *time to get back to the training room*. I often mention it to clients too. I've yet to meet one who isn't, in their own way, a total superstar, yet the vast majority arrive to see me feeling anything but.

The reasons for that are varied, but often they're lacking in confidence to take their next career step and measuring their worth from external accolades. Whether that's praise from a colleague or winning an award, we often think these things will make us feel confident. It's like a sugar rush; great while it lasts, but often short-lived, with a huge crash at the end. While it's great to win awards, in my case everything from the CDI's private sector Career Coach of the Year (2023) to Miss Oakdene (holiday park) beauty contest in 1989 (yes, I do still have the trophy; yes, there is something VERY wrong about a society that judges eight-year-olds on their looks), the real truth, however, is that these are not who I truly am. They don't make me, me.

In today's digital world, social media also fuels constant comparison, feeding our inner critic and fear of not belonging. For women especially, this is reinforced from an early age by media shaping expectations, from how we 'should' look to how to bring up our own children. With so much external noise, it's no wonder people lose touch with or hide who they truly are.

Rather than chasing external validation, we need to support clients in reconnecting with their unique inner selves. Many come to sessions focused on the 'right' job title, but as CDPs, our role is to help them pause and reflect inward. We can hold up a mirror to their strengths, encouraging self-awareness and confidence. Tools and frameworks can support this process but they should never lead it. Use them with intention, always aligned with the client's goals. This work must remain client-led, with tools enhancing reflection, not dictating direction. We can then support clients to shake off the noise of society and manage transitions like puberty, pregnancy, failed fertility, menopause, and so on, where women can lose a sense of who they are. We can support clients to look inside and ask, 'Who are you now?' and then, 'What do you want?' Maybe you knew before, maybe you never did, but you can learn now.

Self-awareness

Society tells women to be quiet and keep small, so although they tend to be more introspective and self-aware, they may have spent many years suppressing who they truly are. One of our first roles then can be digging through their blockers to find what lies beneath. And that bedrock underneath is made up of her own unique set of experiences; life events, relationships, previous roles, the list is endless.

Intersectionality also plays a part in who we think we are. This happens at a very early age and often gets reinforced – for girls they're praised for being a good girl (maybe sitting quietly, for example), and stereotypes of what career a girl is 'allowed' to do are ingrained from early on. Supportive challenge is important here:

- You say you're always rubbish at Maths, what evidence do you have for 'always'?
- You've said your mother is a doctor and you'd also like to do that. What is it that personally appeals to you about this role? Have you considered other options as well?
- Reflect back on what is being said – using their specific words. This shows you're actively listening and building rapport, and there could also be significance in those specific words.
- Also note what is not being said, or what the client doesn't want. Sometimes tapping into why they're not interested in something, or

actively avoid it, can be a way of discovering their inner psyche and values.

● However, tread carefully. Self-awareness and self-esteem are closely linked. If someone is suffering with self-esteem issues, you need to support and help conquer those, in order for them to confidently explore their authentic self. This can be particularly challenging if hormones are causing issues or that person is being made to feel 'other' for any reason.

Be aware that another challenge here is women are often chastised for their emotions, which are linked very directly to a sense of self. Men are rarely given feedback on their behaviours and emotions but for women it's often the key focus, and often negatively so. So should women be 'emotional' at work if they want to progress? Emotions should not be seen as a weakness, but a powerful tool for both women *and* men, and it's these emotions that produce a richness at work, which we shouldn't shy away from as there are benefits for individuals and those who employ them. As Jo Phillips puts it, 'Women should be emotional, as should all humans: it's how we function; it's who we are.' As a society we need to shift our thinking to make emotions a good thing, and as CDPs we can help women show they don't need 'looking after' because they have emotions, quite the opposite. It's these which drive them forward, look at things from different perspectives, and make innovative decisions.

Having a society that tells you not to be emotional can be another thing that keeps women quiet. But we need to encourage women to speak up, use their voice, and fight against the idea of not 'being a Karen'. But using your voice doesn't mean you have to be loud. It's OK if you're not. As an MBTI Practitioner, I find using things like Myers Briggs or one of the other psychometric profiling tools available can be really beneficial. I know on my own journey, I found I gained lots of confidence in understanding a bit more about my drivers, where I get energy from, and my preferences for doing things in certain ways. It made sense of a lot of situations. And Lucy Marie Hornsby had a similar experience. 'Using a psychometric tool really helped me rethink what my strengths are, and another helped me understand why I struggled with certain things. I believe all employers should provide career coaches, but in the absence of them, this sort of thing really helps.'

Values

One of the benefits of tapping into emotions is that particularly strong ones can indicate your values. These are part of what makes you, you. And understanding those provides a roadmap to your authentic self; they're like the compass to show you the way. Katherine Jennick, RCDP, agrees, 'Values are like our guiding light; they're telling us our "why". When you align your personal values with the work you do, that's where the magic happens.'

Values are also the basis of all your actions (even when you don't realise it at the time), and if you can identify and understand them, they help with decision-making. You'll have confidence in yourself and your decisions; procrastination will be eliminated as you understand the rationale behind decisions and can confidently drive forward.

So that all sounds straightforward, why then would you need a CDP's help to explore your values? Often they can be hard to spot because:

- They're so ingrained within you, you don't see them, or don't realise they are unique to you. If being kind is a strong value, you might assume everyone feels the same, but they don't necessarily. And you are a unique blend of all the values you hold, not just one.
- Values are often linked to feelings and emotions, which women have been chastised for, so may shy away from.
- Societal pressures can also cause women to live an inauthentic life. It's not always easy to cut through the noise, to find out what true values lie beneath.
- Your client may simply have never thought about it before. It's only at age 2–4 months that babies fully 'discover' their hands, although they've always been there. Values can be much the same, important yet undiscovered.
- Many of the clients I work with have an internal war going on. They are living, or trying to live a life of 'success', but they've never really sat down and assessed what success looks like to them personally. Often they're trying to fit a mould that isn't right for them. Katherine agrees, 'A lot of people are more successful than they think they are, because maybe they're actually meeting what they deem a success but they've not stopped and thought about it. Once you tick that criteria, you feel more successful and ultimately more confident.' And the foundation for this success criteria is what values you hold most closely to your heart.

Values can also conflict with each other, and the idea of what success looks like can vary by generations. I often see with Gen Z clients that their values of wanting to do good in the world can be in direct conflict with their desire to earn a decent salary, as often these types of roles do not pay well. Farrah Morgan also notes that they feel behind due to COVID, politics, and the economic situation, all impacting the world of work and their progress (or lack of) into and within it. Their focus is often on the here and now or career progression, and, as Farrah highlights, 'I don't really hear a lot on values of flexibility or thinking forward to them being parents, as it's so early in their career for them'.

So what else does matter to them? Farrah highlights the impact of digitalisation on people's lives, and the variety of presentations of success that can be seen online including around:

- Money;
- Careers;
- Businesses people are launching.

'There can be so much overwhelm of how well they "could" be doing, but also feeling like their own prospects are so low.' She notes, as I have also seen with my own clients, that there seems to be a trend that certain pockets of Gen Z feel they are completely stuck. They feel they have no prospects; it is impossible to get on in their career without experience, while they have high expectations of what they want.

Farrah believes that a crucial role she plays is acknowledging the facts of reality (difficult economy, property, and careers ladders both challenging, disparity in society, etc.) but provide some balance. 'Dismantle this belief that they don't have any agency. When they invest in their employability skills they don't fundamentally change as candidates but the way they frame themselves, talk about themselves, radically changes, and then their prospects change as well.' And a great place to start with this is looking at values.

Identify values

Identifying values is indeed important for all clients. For CDPs helping their clients with this, I'm going to bring out the iceberg metaphor once again! Yes, it's important to remember that behaviours, actions, and conversations are often all the metaphorical above water-level iceberg. Our role is to dig into the unconscious and extract the bit of the iceberg that often sits below the water:

someone's values. This can be tough for some, so building psychological safety is important, and encouraging different ways of talking about values could include:

- Using metaphors.
- Talking about people or jobs they admire and reflecting on what that tells them about their values.
- Asking questions about when they've been in flow at work, or when they've felt uncomfortable – exploring why and linking to potential values that they display.
- Showing lists of values and asking clients to point out the ones that resonate with them and then discussing that further.
- Using the golden coaching question 'Anything else?' will also help you dig deeper, to those forgotten/so ingrained values that may not instantly be discussed.
- Katherine Jennick also suggests approaching career choice as 'what problem do you want to solve?' rather than, 'what do you want to do?' This can be an excellent way of getting to the heart of someone's values.
- Understanding Edgar Schein's career anchors model, which includes anchors such as autonomy, security, and service, can help individuals identify the internal motivators that drive their career choices (Schein, 1990). Motivators and values are inherently linked.

It's helpful here to focus on all the values, without doing too much censoring. Only once you have a list, can you then follow this up with activities including:

- Rating each value on a numerical scale, from extremely important to unimportant.
- Ranking them in relation to each other. What feels more important than others.
- Discussing where these values are/are not currently showing up in their life, and then assessing what that means. Is it down to lack of opportunity, suppressing these genuine desires, or lack of knowledge, and so on? Where could the client add some of these – even in small steps/stages?
- Assessing current job (and/or previous ones) – are your values being met? How does that feel?
- Mapping values to any potential future plans/ideas for a career – will they be met? This can be particularly useful if a client is debating between career options.

Another key reason for understanding your values, what they are and what they truly mean to you, is so you can clearly express them to others. Katherine shared stories from her work with young people, including one student who was struggling to write her personal statement. It wasn't until she took the time to explore her values, what mattered to her and why, that she could genuinely articulate her motivations for choosing that course. Providing space for self-reflection is essential, especially for young people, who may not have been taught how to reflect as it helps them connect with their values in a meaningful way.

But are they *really* their values?

It's important, however, that CDPs don't just take values at face, well, value. Especially for women and girls, who have a lot of noise about their expected values, they may not always be showing their authentic ones. As part of your detective stance, active listening, picking out things like 'shoulds' for example, 'I should get a job that pays well' – suggests more about expectations, and less about true values.

A good example I've had many times is a client whose dream career aligns with their values, but it's one that won't pay their bills. Big dreams vs paying the mortgage. What you do here includes:

- Exploring options – for example, a portfolio career to achieve the balance of doing the thing you love and something perhaps you don't but that goes towards the bills. Or it acts as a financially secure stepping stone to the dream.

- Walking a career timeline is a great way to help clients explore decisions in a physical, embodied way. Get them to stand at one end, as if they were five years in the future, and imagine what life looks and feels like if they took a job just for the money. What are the positives, negatives, and what have they said yes or no to? Then repeat the same with the dream job that aligns with their values but pays less. Use chairs or markers to symbolise different decision points: the crossroads, the paid job, the dream job, and guide them through what they notice at each stage. This helps clarify what really matters to them vs what they've been told should matter. For women especially, it can help shift focus back to their own values rather than others' needs. See Tools for more.

- You can also write down each job on a separate piece of card. Rank them against each other for how well they meet the criteria of values, pay, and so on. And then see which comes out on top or what else you can learn from moving the roles around.

Boundaries

For some clients, they may not be living their values, not because they don't know them, but because they are not protecting their boundaries. This could be anything from work/life balance and what that looks like for them, or how much they have to travel for work. I once had a client who was looking for IT jobs and wasn't getting very far. After some exploration into their values we discovered they were struggling as they didn't want to work all the hours, as is often required of the video game companies they were looking into, so they simply shifted the companies/sector they were looking at. They also had a clear boundary of not working for any company involved with the military and so they also set that boundary in place. Using the career path activity from above can help here, if a client is having trouble establishing what their boundaries are, ask how it would feel if they didn't have that boundary in place, what would that look and sound like?

Goals

Why else are values so important? Well, because they are intrinsically linked with our goals. If a client sets a goal and doesn't achieve it, it's often likely because it hasn't met/satisfied one of their values and therefore they've not been motivated to push forward and achieve that goal. So asking 'what is your why?' for goals helps to identify values. If you can identify values, you can identify the purpose of the goal and therefore how likely or not it can be achieved. This isn't just about propelling your client forward, it's about building confidence as goals can be achieved and stopping low self-esteem because of unachieved goals. The client isn't the problem, the goal is! It's not that they can't achieve things, it's because they're picking the wrong things to try and achieve.

This can be done at micro level – such as small goals or steps – or linking that to the bigger concept of a career matching your values and motivators. 99% of the time I talk to clients who are feeling unhappy in their work – it's because the organisation or sometimes the specific manager, whose values do not align with their own. Or they've drifted, often successfully, and now their values are coming to the surface more – maybe things have shifted with time, for example, after having children, or parents passing away, or the ramifications of the pandemic, or hormones – and now the values don't align. Values have probably been there from birth, but sometimes they can develop or shift just like requirements, for example, flexible working because of a family. I never would have thought of flexible working when I was younger, but now I see it aligned to my values of common sense and inclusivity.

Strengths

Values and goals, hopes and dreams, they're all great but they don't really mean anything unless we can achieve them. And we do that by utilising our inner strengths, building our skills, and bringing those together to form competencies. People often mix these up but they're not quite the same. Skills can be things you're naturally good at or things you've learned, strengths are the qualities or talents that come most naturally to you, and competencies are about how you bring your skills and strengths together to perform well in a certain role or situation. Knowing the difference can really help when talking about what you bring to the table.

Helping clients identify and build on their core strengths is one of the key ways CDPs can make a real difference, particularly to female clients who are often not well known for knowing or sharing their strengths. We can support them in bringing those strengths into the light and figuring out how to grow them further. Again, I find psychometric tools really helpful for this, giving clients insight into their strengths, blind spots, what energises them, and what drains them. It can be a powerful way to understand why a job or workplace might not feel like the right fit (instead of defaulting to the common 'I must not be good enough' mindset, so commonly seen in women), and it's just as valuable when preparing for future roles or interviews. Of course, MBTI isn't the only option; there are loads of great profiling tools out there to help clients uncover what might be going on beneath the surface. Ayo Sobo-Keane is also a fan of these kinds of tools, saying they're great for building self-awareness and that it's important as women to have 'as many bits of armour in your toolkit as possible'. Strengths can be absolute gold dust, but only if they're seen and recognised.

Indeed, Katherine Jennick, known in the CDP community for her strengths-based work, believes these skills are often buried and can come from any part of life. 'One of the things that's important is we just shine a light on our everyday lives, because that's where our strengths are.' And many of these may fly under the radar, as they don't have to be huge, incredible things. As Katherine points out, they come from 'everyday life, activities, lived experiences, all make our own unique set of skills and qualities, but as they're part of everyday life, people don't always recognise them'.

So how do we shine a light on our clients' strengths? Top tips include:

- Do an energy audit – ask your client to keep a log for a week, noting down levels of satisfaction and energy on a scale of 1–10. Then explore with them what that tells them about their natural strengths, learned strengths, and development areas.

- List out achievements – I find it's psychologically helpful to step away from the CV and grab a blank piece of paper, but then ask the client to list all the things they are proud of or have achieved in their working life, however big or small. Then discuss what skills and strengths this may be showing and development areas. I've done this particularly with female returner clients, mothers who have been out of paid work for a long time but have been working full-time looking after their children, developing skills and strengths they can apply to the workplace. This activity helps them build confidence in their abilities and moves away from the 'well I've just been a mum' rhetoric.

- Note your behaviours – strengths don't just show up at work. Ask your client to start making a note of the things they are making time for (in and out of work) and things they are avoiding. This behaviour can be very telling about their strengths and development areas, and can surface in both work- and home-life.

- Seek feedback – although we want to strengthen a client's internal monologue, there is nothing wrong with seeking feedback from others to see how they are showing up. What do they see that the client doesn't? This doesn't just have to be long, complicated feedback forms; it can be as simple as 'what three words would you use to describe me?'. See where patterns emerge, ask clients how they feel about the feedback they've received, what resonates, and so on. Nearly 100% of my clients look at me in horror when I suggest this, but absolutely 100% come back beaming from what they've heard.

- Katherine also suggests asking the client to reflect, for example, with a young person, what would your best friend say about you?

She also suggests making it fun, from getting adult clients to WhatsApp friends and family to see what responses they get from a strengths-based question, to teams passing pieces of paper with a person's name and adding their strengths, which then becomes a keepsake. She adds, 'If we can start to normalise talking about our strengths, it feels less like showing off when we do.' This is particularly important for women.

Super strengths

We've all had times when you feel like you've got all your ducks (and the odd pigeon) in a row and things are going well. Maybe you've completed a project in super-quick time or absolutely smashed a presentation. The likelihood is that during these times you've been working in flow. This is when you're immersed and focused on a task, where time feels like it disappears and you're performing at your best. It's that sweet spot where your skills match the challenge, making the work feel energising and effortless.

It's also likely that it's involved using your super strengths. Super strengths are typically defined as your standout qualities, the ones you excel at and that energise you. What makes them 'super' isn't just high performance, but the fact that they feel authentic and are consistently used at your best. Unlike regular strengths (which you might use well but find draining or neutral), super strengths leave you feeling more alive and in flow. This idea is rooted in positive psychology, especially the work of Alex Linley. Super strengths are the top-tier ones that really define how you thrive. So they're obviously great for CDPs to help their clients identify. Many ways you can do this, including the same activities you did for identifying values, but this time for strengths and then highlighting the 'super strengths'. You're also likely to hear about these from others, so getting that strengths feedback is super important.

In addition to helping clients discover their strengths, you can also use strengths-based coaching as a technique to support.

If you feel you don't fit

As well as being more self-aware of values and strengths, we'll look in the next chapter at how you then sell these to businesses with your personal brand. One thing to keep in mind, however, is when women hold themselves back.

For example, not applying for roles unless they meet a significant percentage of the criteria, or shying away from 'manly' descriptors. A useful activity is to help clients map their skills, strengths, and values to either current or potential future job opportunity competencies. You can also take the words they use to describe these and match them against more 'manly' words and reflect on how that then feels.

Summary

For women battling societal expectations, they are not always living their true and authentic selves. Working with a CDP or using the tools in this book and others such as psychometric profiling can help a woman dig into her inner psyche to discover her:

- Values (what really matters and a guiding light to shine the career path);
- Strengths (what she's great at … and super strengths, what she's even better at);
- Goals – and what motivates her;
- How to set boundaries around these.

Tools

We've already covered a lot of actual tools in the chapter, but here are some more.

Coaching questions

- What skill in your life would you most like to improve? How would you decide when you were 'good enough'?
- Imagine you wake up in your dream life. What does that look/ sound/feel like?
- What five words would your best friend use to describe you? What about your worst enemy? What can you learn from this?
- If no one was looking, who would you truly be? Does that change if specific people are looking and why?

- Write a list of all the things you love doing (inside and outside of work). How often do you do them?
- What really matters to you?

Empty chair exercise

A major barrier to identifying strengths and even values is the inner critic. Using the two-chair technique from Gestalt coaching methodology, clients can externalise this voice and better understand its impact. The client speaks to an empty chair as if it were their inner critic, then switches seats to respond from its perspective. This process often creates powerful insight, helping clients move past self-doubt and explore their strengths with greater freedom. If your appointment is online, our friend the Post-it note can work here – wearing one which says 'me' and another which says 'inner critic' can be a chair substitute.

Working in flow

When we're 'working in flow' it's likely that we are linking in some way to our values and/or strengths. Examples can be reviewed from both work situations and home-life (e.g., I am often in flow when carrying out crafting activities, which tap into my inner values and strengths around creativity).

Ask clients:

Think of a time when you were working in flow.

- Where were you?
- Who were you with?
- What was important about this situation?
- What skills/strengths were you using? What were you not using?
- What could you feel/see/hear/think at the time?

Carry out this activity with at least two more examples and then support your client to review the commonalities. What might this suggest to them about their values and strengths?

Drawing 'perfect'

One of my favourite activities during MBTI Practitioner training was drawing our ideal work environment (not necessarily an office). It was surprisingly revealing. Some people included lots of noise, collaboration, and buzz, while others craved peace and quiet. This simple exercise can quickly uncover what someone values in a workplace, offering insight into their core values.

Drawing also taps into a different part of the brain than writing or talking, and can 'free up' the mind to think of alternative ideas. Reassure clients they don't need to be artistic to do this; it's not about how good the picture is but what it tells us. Keep them going by gently prompting with, 'Anything else?' when they pause, or using Clean Language-style questions like, 'What kind of space is that?' or 'Anything else about that space?' You can also ask questions like, 'What kind of work feels so enjoyable it doesn't feel like work?' or 'What would a great working day look like?' These prompts help deepen the reflection and bring valuable insights to the surface. Using words like 'ideal' or 'great' here is better than 'perfect', which can pile on the pressure and feel unmanageable or unattainable.

Practical activities

If some of these activities feel too 'fluffy' for your client, there are more practical options. One is to review job descriptions or career frameworks for roles they've done or are interested in. Help them map their strengths against these – where do they align, what excites them, and why? I like printing them and getting out the pens and highlighters, but you can also do this online.

Another useful tool is the career timeline. Ask your client to visualise or draw a line representing their career journey. Then, have them identify three to five key moments, positive or negative, and talk through why those points stand out. What was happening at the time? Who was involved? What strengths were they using? What values were being challenged? You can also ask them to consider what they now know, or have, that would have helped back then. This reflection can reveal hidden strengths, growth over time, and recurring values or motivators.

Chapter 7
What do people say when you walk out the room?

Like many of my clients, I left university with no real idea what I wanted to do. I read an article about town regeneration and thought it sounded interesting. I had no idea how to get into it, but figured estate agency might be a start. So, with no experience and no driver's licence, I blagged my way into a job.

Two weeks in, I realised I hated it.

Luckily, they moved me into marketing. Turns out creativity, not sales, was more my thing, and I enjoyed it. But the culture was awful. So I did the only thing that made sense at the time: I quit and went travelling.

I'd found an organisation that brought solo travellers together. We were given each other's emails (this was dial-up days, no smartphones, no socials), and at first, the messages were all polite: 'Hi, nice to meet you', 'Excited but nervous', and so on. Sweet, but eventually dull.

So I tried something different: I introduced myself by sending 20 random questions. Would you rather fly or be invisible? If you were an animal, what would you be? (A flying giraffe, obviously.)

Suddenly, departure day had arrived. The walls of Heathrow were reverberating with the excitement of the group as everyone introduced themselves. I only had to say my name once. 'Ah! You're the questions girl! I was looking forward to meeting you!'

That, my friends, is personal brand.

And in a crowded job market, whether you're helping a client to find a new role or progress within their current company, supporting them to develop their own 'personal brand' will help them be seen, heard, and understood, giving them the edge over the competition. It's like if I said to you 'golden arches' or 'never knowingly undersold', you'd know what brands I was talking about and what they stood for. It's just as important for individuals, even those employed by others, to become liked, known, and trusted for the things they're brilliant at. They introduce them before they even introduce themselves, getting them a foot in the door and driving forward their career.

So what does a personal brand look like? As Jeff Bezos once famously put it, 'Your brand is what people say about you when you walk out the room.' Vicki Knights, a brand photographer and positive psychology practitioner, also stressed that your brand is what you choose as 'a way you're recognised and remembered. It's how you intentionally bring together your unique values, skills, and characteristics in order to fulfil your purpose.'

Authenticity is key here; if a client is not comfortable with the brand they're creating, others won't engage with it. They can still push themselves before they're ready, or go in a different career direction, but they need to focus on what makes you, you, and how that translates for the path ahead. That can be hard to work out and so Vicki suggests flipping it on its head: 'Ask yourself, "What would you hate people to say about you when you're not in the room?"' Or a copywriter I once worked with encouraged me to look through all the client feedback I had received, noting common words/themes that emerged. This is great to encourage clients to do, whether it's client feedback or 360 reviews from colleagues; it will give them a sense of how they are showing up to others. And whether that's the way they want to or not.

Why it matters

As we've seen throughout the book, women have a harder 'sell' to convince others of their worth. There are many further nuances to this, including age discrimination. As shown in a 2023 research report by Professor Ian Burn, which showed that women begin facing age discrimination in the hiring process from around age 40, at least a decade earlier than men (Burn, 2023). The research highlighted how gender and age intersect to disadvantage older women in the labour market, with significantly lower callback rates for job applications submitted by older female candidates. So a strong brand, which emphasises the unique value that the individual adds, is crucial for career confidence and success.

Sadly, it isn't any easier for women at the start of their careers either, again highlighting the need for a personal brand. Ayo Sobo-Keane points out that 'as women, you have to try harder at most things and you have to give yourself the best opportunities. So if that's personal branding, the earlier in your career you can establish that, the better. It's more natural to you and you've grown into it. It's imperative for young women starting out their work journey and helps build confidence.'

Another advantage of establishing your personal brand is that it helps you establish your core offer. As Vicki highlights, 'Working on your personal brand helps you identify that main thing and gives you clarity on what you really want to be known for.' This then puts you in the driving seat, instead of staying small and therefore missing opportunities. Making your brand known and getting visible, as Vicki puts it, 'just means that rather than constantly having to chase opportunities, they're much more likely to fall into your lap'. This can give women the edge in a competitive job and career market and build their confidence in the process.

When we talk about 'getting visible' what does that mean? We're not talking about being an influencer here; it's about not hiding behind work or talents, but supporting the individual to shine. For women, that could look like:

- Putting your hand up for new projects;
- Working with others outside your usual team;
- Posting thought leadership ideas on LinkedIn or sharing the success you've had. It can even be sharing the 'failures' and what you've learned from them;
- Volunteering on boards or other groups, for example, your professional body;
- Speaking at company meetings;
- Raising your hand and asking pertinent questions at those meetings;
- Putting yourself forward for speaking opportunities;
- Appearing in publications, books, podcasts;
- Taking part in volunteering with schools, for example, at careers events, and then sharing about it on social media;
- Mentoring others or being mentored by senior members of the company.

And CDPs can help their clients explore all of these options and opportunities.

Developing an individual brand

There are five core elements to developing a brand for moving forward within a career, and CDPs can help their clients to assess all of them:

1. Core strengths and skills.
    Your personal brand is selling you, so you need to show what you're good at. See chapter 6 for more on how to identify these.

2. Values and purpose.
    Your brand should reflect what you stand for, and why. It's about what motivates you and drives you forward.

3. Career vision and goals.
    Linked to this motivator is a clear vision of where you're heading. Your brand should reflect not only where you are now, but, more importantly, where you want to be. This helps manifest future opportunities and solidifies you as the person who is liked, known, and trusted for that thing. A lot of this will be about sharing transferable skills, experiences, and a thirst for more/having the right attitude for the future.

4. Unique Selling Point (USP).
    Yes, it's not just companies that need this. Imagine you're going for a job, you're down to the final two – why should they hire you over anyone else? You're a unique mixture of talent and experiences, and you need to put these forward. I often work with clients who feel they are a 'jack of all trades', but I believe this is their USP; it's the specific mixture of experience they have.

5. Tone and personality.
    Many of my clients are terrified of LinkedIn. They feel they shouldn't go on there unless they have something terribly clever and professional to say. It reminds me of my brother-in-law's advice when I was first asked to speak on the *BBC News* for A Level results day: 'Don't try and be clever, just be you.' Luckily I know him well enough to know he wasn't being rude; he just knows my brand. As the book highlights, my brand is supportive, helpful, practical; not theory-based academia. And that's what people buy into as it's authentically me. Support your clients to be unashamedly themselves, and make sure their personality shows up in their personal brand.

Vicki also highlights another area CDPs can help: checking in with their clients that their brand is actually their authentic self and not what they've been told they 'should' have. 'Quite often, they've been told by their company they're too this or that. But this isn't about moulding them to fit that company, it's about helping them discover who they are as their authentic self.' Likewise, when I work with self-employed people, they worry if their brand doesn't reach everyone, but that's the point; you don't want it to. An authentic brand should connect authentically with others where you'll be the right 'fit'. A brand, whether the person is self-employed looking for customers or searching the job market for employment, should detract those who won't serve you as much as those who will. This all links back to a client's values and purpose.

And as Lee Gilbert also points out, sometimes you can garner praise for the brand you're showing, but it isn't always authentically you, and that doesn't feel great. 'I used to do a lot of speaking before my transition, and people said I was good at it. But I was using muscle memory of societal norms, from tone of voice to body language, and internally I was putting myself in a position every time and that became very challenging.'

Ongoing assessment

This is also not just a one-time conversation. There are many points where a personal brand may not feel like the right fit anymore. For women in particular, who go through many transitions in their life, from puberty to pregnancy and perimenopause and beyond, they can often feel like they lose themselves a little. Lee also explained that after her transition, she took time to re-evaluate her personal brand, and 'that did take me a while to figure out, having a personal brand and having an ability to connect some sort of confidence to that. I'd become overly conscious of how to express confidence as a trans woman versus my sex assigned at birth, and how that looked as my personal brand.'

CDPs can help their clients (re)discover who they are and bring back their sparkle and ensure their brand aligns. Or even assist them when they look to change careers, as the career that worked for 20-year-old them does not work for 40-plus-year-old them. Spending time on re-establishing their brand will then assist them when it comes to being visible, and, as Vicki puts it, 'it's not just about showing up as you always have. It's about helping clients find new, authentic ways to show up that feel right for them.' I always find when clients are comfortable with their brand, they're more comfortable getting visible.

They also need to be comfortable with how they get visible, and again CDPs can help them work through this and establish what works authentically for them. Vicki agrees and believes there are ways to build up to visibility if a client is unsure about this, at any point in their career. CDPs can help clients review:

- Where do you feel most yourself at work? Is it certain tasks or with certain people? How could you show more of that in your brand?

- Don't leap out of your comfort zone – take a small step. Perhaps don't stand on stage in front of hundreds of people, but speak to the marketing team about being a spokesperson for press articles coming out. Start with something small that feels manageable.

- Ask yourself how you would show up if you didn't care what people thought? Then ask yourself what steps you could take towards doing whatever that thing is.

- Cheryl Insley, a personal stylist, also adds that if you're looking for a further confidence boost, 'we can change how we feel internally by what we wear. Clothing is a really powerful tool, it's not just surface level, it's about controlling our narrative and what makes you feel confident walking into a room.'

Bragging rights

However it's done, it's good that a brand gets shared, and often. The more it is, the more an individual will get comfortable with what it is and how to share it, including:

- Hone the message – get crystal clear on what it is and how to portray it.

- Increase confidence – sharing this new brand can cause us to lose confidence; we worry about failure or being laughed at. But the more comfortable you get with it, the more your confidence builds.

- Practice makes perfect – both in everyday situations and specifics like interviews.

But the problem is, if we share how brilliant we are, this feels a bit like bragging. After all, nobody likes a show-off, do they? With a lifetime of hearing from society, other people, and the media about what it is to be 'likeable' as a woman, that we mustn't be 'too much', it's no wonder that, as Vicki puts it, 'women naturally make themselves smaller in order to be liked and accepted'.

But here's the thing. It's not bragging if it's based on evidence. And as CDPs, we can support our clients by looking at their values, their skills, their strengths, and looking at examples to back these things up … and there is a personal brand right there. And Vicki suggests that if we focus our brand and visibility 'as the impact we want to have rather than thinking of it as I'm being visible, because I want to show off and tell everyone how brilliant I am', then this can encourage women to get more comfortable with it.

We can also encourage the women we work with to share their voice. There is a lot of confidence building we need to do here, and as Vicki says, encouraging clients to understand that 'visibility isn't about showing up because we're perfect, or we want to be famous, or we think we know everything. It's just because our voices matter. And we want to make an impact on people.'

This does not come naturally to many women, who feel the need to be perfect before speaking up. I've experienced this with many of my clients, and in talking to lots of other women for the book they've experienced the same, that clients feel they need to be an expert before they speak up. And they don't just need to be an expert, they need to be the best expert, the most experty-expert there ever was. But the reality is, they'll never feel like that; there will always be some part of their internal monologue, and no doubt external noise, which will encourage them to think they're not perfect. Because nobody is. As CDPs, our role is to encourage clients to understand they are perfectly them, and that's someone the world needs to see and hear. And the more we can hold that space of psychological safety and non-judgement, to help individual women to be brave, to develop their brand and to make it visible to others, the more those others will feel it's ok to share theirs. It's part of the power and the privilege of the work we do; it has a far greater reach than we often realise or talk about. Maybe we ourselves need to work more on that, the brand for our sector, but that's another book(!)

Brand sharing

Telling a client to 'be visible' is as helpful as 'be confident'; well-intentioned but with no direction, ultimately useless. As well as living their brand, they also need to reinforce that, to ensure it is seen, heard, understood, and valued. You'll find some ways to do that on the following pages.

Storytelling/crafting your narrative

We've all had to sit through painfully dull presentations that promised so much and delivered so little. But you know what? I once went to a thrilling talk about, wait for it … GDPR! Yes, really (apologies to the GDPR geeks out there but it's not what excites most of us). But why was that session so good? Because the presenter used storytelling.

You don't have to be a presenter on stage to make use of storytelling; it's a great way in any conversation, social media post, and your wider brand to craft your narrative. It's a way to engage people, to make them want to know more, to buy into whatever you are 'selling' (you!). There are many models out there on how to frame your story. One of the most common is that of the 'Hero' – 'I faced a problem that you're having too, I tried all the options but nothing worked, then I found this one simple hack and suddenly it all became a breeze, and now I am a successful billionaire with a lavish lifestyle. And I have the magic to help you achieve this too.'

This is just one of many similar models, often used by businesses but can be employed by individuals seeking career growth as well. So whether they're self-employed, looking for employment, or developing in their current career, or even pivoting, selling a story is a great way to engage others. Individuals can selectively use parts of their career history to show their 'new' focused brand. Selecting which parts of their career they want in their brand can actually be a good career exploration activity in itself. CDPs can help here, along with helping to craft this into a strong message. You could do this through coaching questions, or activities such as writing the anecdotes onto individual cards/Post-its and then lining up which match the new brand and which don't. If digital is your thing, then you can do the same on platforms such as Trello, Padlet, or Notion.

It's worth noting that CDPs can draw on the DOTS model (Decision-learning, Opportunity-awareness, Transition-learning, Self-awareness) – in which storytelling is crucial. Storytelling helps individuals reflect on their experiences, values, and aspirations; make sense of their journey, shape their narrative, and communicate their career motivations and strengths. Together, this forms the heart of their brand storytelling (Law & Watts, 1977).

Katherine Jennick also suggests storytelling as a great way of using Narrative Theory to showcase your strengths and values. 'There's nobody better to tell that story than yourself. You're the main character and the author, so if you can say something from your life, like an event, activity, or lived experience, that is the best way to showcase your strengths and values.' This can be particularly important for young people or women who have taken time off for caring responsibilities and don't have a lot of work experience. Using personal examples and using those to craft their story and weave it into their brand, and how those strengths from home-life could be effective in the workplace, is a very powerful tool.

Elevator pitch

Think of this as the intro to the full story. In a short space of time (length of an elevator ride), a woman needs to show who she is, what she stands for, and her goals. She needs to share her motivators, and why she's good at it (her USP). It's the way to draw people in to engage with her whole story.

CDPs can help here by:

- Reminding clients their USP is just that – unique, even if they think everyone does it, they don't. Review skills and strengths here if needed.
- Map out some examples – don't need to include in the pitch, but it helps set it in the client's mind.
- Ask them to map out some examples of 'when you are at your best you have …'. Often, when we're at our best, it's because we're aligning with our values and strengths, and these should form the basis of an authentic brand and pitch.
- Practice makes perfect – encourage the client to practise, in front of you, even recording it and playing it back. Supportive challenge here as people don't like to be recorded but it can provide great insights when you watch it back. Can also use the 'read aloud' function of Word or AI to get feedback on a pitch script.

Visibility — appearance

This isn't about looks; it's about having confidence in your own skin. Whether someone is walking into an interview, a boardroom, or showing up on LinkedIn with a professional photo, feeling confident and showing that authentic brand is crucial. But how does someone do that when they might not be feeling at their confident best? Cheryl suggests using colours and clothes to help instil that confidence. 'I work with a lot of women who are technically confident in their job, but are feeling a bit lost in themselves. They're busy caring for others; their bodies and lifestyle are changing, so they get lost. But they can use colour, and clothes, to create confidence.'

Just as what we say forms part of our brand, Cheryl also believes that 'colour and style are a language without you talking, they are communicating something'.

So this can form part of a client's brand:

- As a way of establishing they are an 'authority'/want to be taken seriously – particularly important for those early in their career or looking to move up a stage or make a career change.

- As a way of working out a career plan – I once worked with a client in her 20s who wanted to do a job where she had to wear a 'power suit'. Our job here is to unpick this idea and help the client to establish what they mean by that and what that means for their career.

- As a way of pushing themselves out of their comfort zone and trying new things. Much like career steps, which rather than big leaps, are about small steps, Cheryl suggests the client doesn't need to push too far, too quickly. 'Black is a perfectly fine colour to wear but many women hide behind it. Rather than them next wearing a bright blue jump suit, they could start small, adding some brighter accessories.'

- Mo (Mousumi) Kanjilal also shared a story of a coach who'd pointed out that as a sales person she wanted to stand out, so using bright colours in her outfits was a way of doing that.

Cheryl also explains that although she has male clients too, for women 'there is an extra societal pressure from the media, telling them to look a certain way and how they're marketed at which makes them wish they look different, and then asking, "Who are you trying to impress?" On top of that, women are often mothers, have lifestyle changes, like menopause, and what that does to the body etc.'

But it's not all doom and gloom. Cheryl sees clothing as a way for women to define or redefine who they are, to create a wardrobe that works for them now and brings joy. 'This is all about how we can leverage what people actually have and are, rather than focusing on what they don't. In my teenage years I was unconfident, having been so heavily marketed at and wishing I looked different. But the more I embraced who I was, and what I was, and my strengths, the more passionate I became about myself.'

As with imposter thoughts, this is about highlighting positives, not just tackling negatives. It's about helping clients feel confident in their own skin, embrace their authentic selves inside and out, and focus on *them*, not the wider world. That's when they start to live and breathe their personal brand, gaining confidence, agency, and authenticity and drawing the right people to their brand in doing so.

Visibility in and out of the workplace

Clients can use visibility to make sure their brand is reinforced consistently. One question I love to ask is: 'How can you be more visible?' Clients often have one particular method and only stick to that, or have sporadic periods of visibility, but these can be problematic. Vicki agrees, 'You need everyone to see a consistent brand, not all be thinking different things, and you need to be visible to achieve that.'

I had this conversation with a client recently. She'd been speaking up in meetings but wasn't sure that was working for her. We explored whether her contributions were building her brand or just coming across as interruptive. Then we brainstormed other ways she could show up, from joining cross-functional projects to speaking at company-wide meetings.

When you're not sitting next to your manager, their manager, or your colleagues, how do you make a name for yourself and show off your brand? Again, with a history of women being told to keep quiet, not make a fuss or bother anyone, it can be tough. So help your client find comfortable ways of doing this, whether it's messaging people via chat, taking part in work social events, or something else that fits their style. I often find psychometric profiling tools help clients figure out what kind of visibility approach works best for them.

For women who brand themselves as 'shy' or just simply more introverted, standing on a stage might not be the right way for them to get visible. CDPs can help here, tapping into the psychometric profiling to understand their strengths and where and how they can be visible. For example, tapping into their abilities to make deeper connections, organising meetings with key people in an organisation, can be a strong way to show their brand. Likewise, they may feel more comfortable reaching out via DM on social media. As long as they can articulate their brand, it's still a great way for them to get visible for the things they're great at.

And however it is done, what that name is that someone is making for themselves matters. Not just in person, but online too. The next time someone goes for a promotion, looks for a new role, or even goes to a meeting with external people, the first thing those people will do is look them up. So encourage clients to look themselves up and see what they find. The fact is, if you're not visible, sharing what *you* want to be known for, the things others will find are what others are saying about you, or old outdated versions of your brand. Vicki summarises it brilliantly when she suggests, 'Make your purpose bigger than your fear.' Next time a client says they're worried what this person or that will think if they speak up in a meeting, or put a post on LinkedIn, ask them, 'What will they think if you don't?'

Summary

A client being good at their job is level 1, but making sure others know it is next level, and CDPs can help. Having a clear brand is essential to help build confidence and get on in the world of work and should include the elements of:

1. Core strengths and skills;

2. Values and purpose;

3. Career vision and goals;

4. Unique Selling Point;

5. Tone and personality.

By establishing these things for oneself early on in a career, individuals can help propel themselves forward with confidence and purpose. It's essential to ensure they don't just know this brand, but others do too, so taking up every opportunity to be visible is really important. This could include anything from a post on LinkedIn to speaking up in a company meeting. The key element is to be your authentic self and ensure that when you walk out of the room, what others are saying about you is what you want them to say.

Tools

Coaching questions

- If you could create a mission statement for your life, what would it be?
- What are you like when you're at your best?
- How do you think others currently perceive you, and how does that align with how you want to be seen?
- If your personal brand were a tagline, what would it be?
- What values and strengths do you want your personal brand to consistently reflect?
- What makes you different?

All in the image

So much of personal branding is about images – whether it's the image you're portraying, or what you're physically wearing. So doing activities which use images here can be helpful. Ask a client to draw out or collage the image they want to portray. You could do this metaphorically – asking clients to pick pictures out of magazines which represent this idea, anything from a wall (representing strength and stability) to an image of a woman, head back laughing, full of confidence. You could also work with a client to literally pick out the kinds of clothes, colours, and so on which they may like to wear. Once they've done this, discuss how this links to their authentic brand – it could also be a way of discovering that brand.

If you think a client isn't ready for this, or struggling to define their brand, it can also be useful to share pictures of other women and ask the client to describe them. See what they're picking out about their ideas of their brand, what resonates, what doesn't, and so on.

What's in YOUR wardrobe?

Sticking with image for the moment, Cheryl suggests asking clients to think about their values and how they want to show up to others. Then head to their wardrobe and think, 'Does the outfit I'm pulling together show this?' Pro tip – look at your own wardrobe – we're (trying!) to move on from the CDP image of little old lady in a cardy; what do your outfits say to your clients? Are you promoting the psychological safety or confidence you want to? Cardies and all, we're here for it!

Vision statement

I spend a lot of time talking to clients about setting them up for their future, which means showing up as that future (even before they're ready). So their brand should be as much about what they want for the future as what they feel they're doing now. In order to achieve that, writing a vision statement can help them to visualise what they want, how they'll get there, and what they 'look' like.

Ask the client to think ahead to six months or three years into the future. Write a vision statement in the present tense, as if it's already happening, which creates a closer connection to it.

- How are you showing up in this vision?
- Who did you need help from to achieve your vision?
- What steps did you take to achieve your vision?

Feedback

As humans, and women in particular, we can struggle to shout about what makes us brilliant. Getting feedback from others, even a simple activity like asking three people to describe you in three words, can be a great platform to build your brand around.

Other ways to help a client identify their values and strengths can include:

- Providing a long and varied list of words and clients pick which ones resonate, then numbering them in terms of those they most strongly associate with, or use, or don't get the opportunity to use can all provide highly useful intel.

- Using card activities to explore strengths, identifying those that resonate, and discussing examples of where they have used them.

- If feedback that a client is getting does not align with their personal brand, a good activity is for them to write all the words they want their personal brand to be in one column, all the feedback words in the other, and if there is a disconnect, discuss why. Is it about them not being visible? Have they been living someone else's brand (i.e., what society or perhaps a previous employer has expected of them), or is it an old brand that now doesn't fit? Knowing where you're at can then be a platform for how to move on to show the brand you want.

SECTION 3
Achieving the success you deserve, now and in the future

Chapter 8
Know your rights

At age three my career plan was to be a ballet dancer. By Year 9 I'd decided a career in law was for me. Why? Probably because my Mum was the practice manager for a firm of solicitors. Like many young people, my career choice was influenced by observational learning of someone close to me, as explained by the Social Learning Theory of Career Decision Making (Krumboltz, 1979). I often talk to young clients about the work experience I did, spending time in the magistrate's court, even watching an accused jump over the barrier and run off; it was thrilling but by the end of the week I'd decided it wasn't the career for me.

Instead, I became a detective. Because that's what CDPs really are, right? Pulling together all the pieces of a client's life and choices, helping them discover things about themselves or the workplace around them, to find the right fit. And our role traverses many others, including solicitors. It's vital to stress to clients we are not legal professionals, but for anyone working with clients to support them with their careers, it's important to have some understanding of legal frameworks that sit within the workplace. In having this basic knowledge, you can help signpost clients to gain further support where required. Clients often don't need, or want, to go down an official legal route, but knowing there are options can be a huge help. As Katherine Watkins, a Magistrate and International HR Professional and Chief People Officer, puts it, 'There's an awful lot of legislation that should be there to protect females. But you've got to know what it is, when to use it, and how to use it. As an HR professional I see applicants who come to court but they've not read the company handbook, policies, or employment law.' Women traditionally are not always great at speaking up and gaining support from others, and as CDPs we can play a role here by encouraging them to do so.

Sadly, however, we're living in a world that can at times have serious consequences for women, from rape and death threats on social media to sexual misconduct at work. Understanding something of the law to support women can be advantageous, and being mindful of both your clients' safety and, particularly for female CDPs, that of your own too. We often operate essentially as lone workers, tucked away in small offices with individuals we've never met before. Whether you're working with young people or adults, speak to your employer or hiring client about safety measures to protect both you and your clients.

This cross-over between career and legal advice is how I first met Charlotte Yallop, an Employment Law Solicitor and Partner. We were both advising a woman on social media who had a question about her career. I was giving some career advice, Charlotte discussing the legal aspects of the situation. So I knew she'd be the perfect person to give an overview of some of the employment law that could impact the careers of women.

Note that while the English judicial system is slow and cumbersome, it does change, so do make sure you are focusing on the most up-to-date and relevant legal advice (with the ongoing rollout of the Employment Rights Act 2025 and the April 2025 ruling of how 'sex' is interpreted under the Equality Act 2010, which may have implications for the women you work with going forward). Here is Charlotte's advice for your clients, quoting the law as of July 2025:

* * *

When it comes to your working life, knowing your rights isn't just about legal safety nets, it's about empowerment. Whether you're entering your first job, navigating pregnancy, balancing caregiving, or planning your next promotion, understanding how the law supports women can help them advocate for themselves or others with confidence.

The basics: What women are entitled to

Every employee and worker in England and Wales has a set of core rights. These apply regardless of whether they're full-time, part-time, permanent, or fixed-term.

Here are the legal minimums/essentials:

- **Minimum wage**: Employees are legally entitled to be paid at least the National Minimum Wage or National Living Wage depending on their age.

- **Paid annual leave**: Most workers are entitled to 5.6 weeks of paid holiday each year (that's 28 days if you work full-time, pro rata for part-time workers and includes public holidays).

- **Rest breaks and working time limits**: Workers are entitled to regular breaks, daily rest between shifts, and a limit on their average weekly working hours unless they opt out.

- **Protection from unfair dismissal**: At present, after two years' continuous service, you can't be sacked without a fair reason and a fair process. Under the Employment Rights Act 2025, the qualifying period will decrease to six months. It is expected that this will apply to employees who have six months' service on 1 January 2027.

- **Right to request flexible working**: Since April 2024, all employees can request flexible working from day one.

- **Family-related leave and pay**: Including maternity, paternity, adoption, and parental leave.

- **Protection from discrimination and harassment**: More on this shortly.

These rights are a legal baseline of non-negotiables. Many employers go further, offering enhanced leave, better pay, or additional support policies, but they can never go below these standards.

What does it mean to be 'protected'?

The law recognises that some groups of people are more likely to face unfair treatment at work, whether because of gender, race, age, or other characteristics. That's why the Equality Act 2010 makes it unlawful to discriminate against someone on the basis of a protected characteristic.

There are nine in total:

1. Sex;

2. Pregnancy and maternity;

3. Race;

4. Disability;

5. Age;

6. Religion or belief;

7. Sexual orientation;

8. Gender reassignment;

9. Marriage or civil partnership.

Being 'protected' doesn't mean you're immune to bias, but it does mean workers have legal grounds to challenge it. Discrimination doesn't always look like blatant sexism, for example. Sometimes it shows up as being left out of projects, getting passed over for promotion after maternity leave, or being penalised for needing flexible hours to care for children. If the reason connects to one of the protected characteristics, it may be unlawful, and you have a right to speak up.

Pregnancy and maternity: Know your rights

From the moment someone tells their employer they're pregnant, they gain legal protections. These include:

- Paid time off for antenatal appointments;
- The right to up to 52 weeks of maternity leave (Ordinary Maternity Leave (OML) covers the first 26 weeks and Additional Maternity Leave (AML) covers the subsequent 26 weeks);
- Statutory Maternity Pay (or Maternity Allowance if you don't qualify) for 39 weeks, with the first 6 weeks at 90% of average weekly earnings and the remaining 33 weeks at either a set rate or 90% of average earnings, whichever is lower;
- Protection from unfair treatment or dismissal because of pregnancy;
- The right to return to their job (after OML), or a suitable alternative (after AML), after maternity leave ends.

If they're made redundant during maternity leave, they must be offered any suitable available job ahead of others. This 'priority status' was extended in 2024 to last for 18 months from the birth or adoption placement.

What many people don't know is that pregnancy and maternity discrimination can occur even before someone takes leave, such as if they're passed over for a promotion after announcing their pregnancy or excluded from development opportunities. This type of behaviour is unlawful. Importantly, you don't need two years' service to be protected from pregnancy or maternity discrimination. It applies from day one. The Employment Rights Act 2025 will provide enhanced support and protection to women who are pregnant or on maternity leave.

Menopause: No law yet, but still protected

There's currently no specific menopause law, but many women are still protected under the Equality Act. That's because severe or long-lasting menopausal symptoms can count as a disability.

This means that if their symptoms substantially affect their ability to do day-to-day tasks and last (or are likely to last) for at least 12 months, their employer must make reasonable adjustments to help them stay in work. This could include:

- Adjusting hours;
- Providing access to fresh air, fans, or uniform changes;
- Allowing more breaks or flexible deadlines;
- Supporting remote or hybrid working.

Even if their symptoms aren't classed as a disability, they could still be protected from sex, age, or disability discrimination, depending on how they're treated.

More and more good employers are introducing menopause-friendly policies, manager training, and dedicated wellbeing support. When job hunting, it's worth checking whether the company mentions menopause in its health or inclusion materials; this can be. a sign of a thoughtful, progressive culture.

Additionally, the Employment Rights Act 2025 includes provisions to improve workplace support for employees experiencing menopause. Key aspects include requiring larger employers to publish menopause action plans.

Flexible working: From day one

Previously, employees had to wait six months before asking for a flexible working arrangement. But from April 2024, every employee is given the right to request flexible working from their first day.

This could include:

- A four-day week;
- Job sharing;

- Earlier or later start times;
- Hybrid or remote working;
- Compressed hours (e.g., doing full-time hours over fewer days).

An employer must deal with the request reasonably and consult the individual before rejecting it. They can only say no for one of eight business reasons (such as impact on performance or costs), but they must give proper thought to your proposal.

If flexible working is refused unfairly, and it particularly disadvantages women (as many rigid policies do), it could even be indirect sex discrimination.

Harassment and workplace culture

Sadly, many women experience inappropriate or uncomfortable behaviour at work, from offhand sexist jokes to intrusive questions or comments. If the behaviour is unwanted, related to a protected characteristic, and creates a hostile, intimidating, or humiliating environment, it may count as harassment under the Equality Act.

Further, since 26 October 2024, employers are under a legal duty to proactively prevent sexual harassment in the workplace. This means that employers must take reasonable steps to prevent sexual harassment of their employees, not just respond to incidents after they occur. Failure to comply with this duty can result in increased compensation for victims of sexual harassment.

Individuals don't need to wait until it becomes unbearable. Often, saying 'That's not OK' early, either directly or through HR, can stop the behaviour. But if the problem continues or is more serious, they have the right to raise a formal grievance and seek legal advice if needed.

Beyond the law: What good employers offer

Many organisations go further than the legal minimum. For example, some voluntary policies that show a company takes women's working lives seriously include:

- Enhanced maternity/paternity leave and pay;
- Fertility and miscarriage leave;

- Paid carers' or emergency dependants' leave;
- Menopause, menstrual, and reproductive health policies;
- Internal networks and mentoring for women;
- Domestic abuse support policies;
- Returner programmes after a career break.

While these aren't legal requirements, they reflect an employer's values. If comparing job offers or thinking of moving on, don't be afraid to ask about them.

What to do if things go wrong

Sometimes things feel off, whether it's a slow slide into being left out, a clash with a manager, or something more serious like discrimination or dismissal. Here's a simple roadmap women can follow if this is the case:

1. **Trust your gut**: If it feels unfair, don't brush it off.

2. **Keep records**: Save emails, take notes of conversations, and write down what happened and when.

3. **Check your policies**: Look up your company's grievance, maternity, flexible working, and equality policies.

4. **Raise it informally first**: Often, a calm conversation with your manager or HR can fix the problem.

5. **Use your grievance procedure**: If not, escalate the issue in writing following your internal policy.

Important: Most employment claims have a three-month time limit from the date of the issue (e.g., the date of the discrimination or dismissal), so acting quickly is important.

* * *

The law vs reality

So that's Charlotte's advice on what the law says, but it's also important to understand that the law isn't always followed to the letter. I delved further into some of these topics with the other women I interviewed, about the actual implications of these laws, whether companies do uphold them, and the impact of this on women's careers.

Protected characteristics

When discussing protected characteristics with Mo (Mousumi) Kanjilal, she felt that it 'does give people some protection, there is the option for taking people to tribunals. But that doesn't necessarily stop people being under attack. If you look at what is happening to the trans community right now, or the stat that 74,000 women a year lose their jobs through maternity discrimination, despite that being protected.' Here Mo is referencing the 2025 report by Pregnant Then Screwed, that approximately 74,000 women in the UK lose their jobs each year due to pregnancy or maternity leave, a stark 37% increase from around 54,000 in 2016.

Ayo Sobo-Keane did, however, observe that 'anything that can be highlighted, then initiates a discussion, and spreads the word. That in itself is a good thing.' And as we have seen throughout the book, for women in particular who tend to internalise things, this could be particularly beneficial for the advancement of their careers.

As we've also seen from Charlotte, while menopause is not officially yet a protected characteristic, there is overlap. So helping clients to look for companies that may be understanding of this is key. Katherine Watkins, however, points out that it's not just about policy; it's about looking into the 'tangibility of how they bring a policy to life'. It's about how they provide information through their EAP (Employee Assistance Programme), bring in their providers or other organisations to help, and run groups or talks for women (and men) to give support. Like with so many of these topics, it's about taking the law, policy, common sense, kindness, and thinking about how that can truly support the women in their organisation. And there are ways women can include a desire for a company that does this into their career management plans, and CDPs can help them with this.

Gender pay gap reporting

As well as the legal obligations for employers which Charlotte explained, there are also some for specific companies. One example of this is gender pay gap reporting, which is a legal requirement for UK employers with 250 or more employees to publish data showing the difference in average earnings between men and women in their organisation. Katherine Watkins explains, 'The ethos is to create a more equal pay structure across sexes. Applicable organisations have to submit data on employee wages. However, there are ways to manipulate the figures, so it can be a disappointingly untrustworthy process.' However, much like Ayo's thoughts on protected characteristics, Katherine did feel that 'having this system in place can cause companies to stop and think, realise they need to be more equal in what they're paying, and that can be good for the individual (who can look the data up)'. Sadly, however, Jo Phillips believes that rather than protecting women, it can have the opposite effect. 'Women are not seen, not appreciated as equals. When an employer also knows their previous salary, when there is likely already a gap between her and male candidates, it's a compelling commercial decision to offer the female a role, on the basis that it helps towards their EDI targets, and the organisation can offer a slightly higher salary to the female, while still low balling and keeping their spend firmly in check.'

However, as well as its challenges, there are some positives. Alongside a potential tool for the individuals, it can also be a tool to support HR. As Katherine points out, they are 'the guardians of fair and transparent pay structures, but when that isn't happening, it can be hard to know how to manage that. Often HR Directors are not able to influence at board level, but this process can support them.' So while not perfect, it is perhaps another tool which employers, and employees, can use to make a more level playing field, but it's surprising the number of individuals who still know nothing about this. In addition, the Employment Rights Act will bring greater expectations of employers around gender pay reporting. Again, here is an area where CDPs having this knowledge can help support their clients in their career management skills.

Another area CDPs can help clients is with their confidence with, and the skill of, negotiation. As Jo explains, for many women this does not always come easily. 'This is often on the basis that if they can see a trade-off between salary and working flexibly (as they are likely to be expected to be the main or primary carer for the next generation), they will acquiesce to the slightly lower salary, assuming that they can't have everything. The truth is she can have it all, she just can't do it all, and this is why the higher salary is key, she will need help to raise her family and she can't do it without the income.' Aside from negotiation skills, Jo also believes that as careers professionals, we can support our clients by encouraging them not to share current or previous salaries. 'Employers find it incredibly hard to low ball an offer if they don't know her previous earnings, which is where the #makesalaryhistory campaign comes in. In essence this bans employers from asking salary questions at any stage in the application process. Interestingly, as of June 2026, EU employers will not legally be allowed to ask this.'

Culture and the law

Whatever the area of law, one thing is certain, and that is if you can find the right company culture, it makes things a lot easier. For example, as Ruth McAteer puts it, 'The law is frequently not followed, and inherent bias exists. The emphasis is on women with disabilities to bring an employer to task, rather than on the employer to create inclusive spaces. Law is not enough, the culture needs to be one of inclusion, not because they have to, but because they want to.' CDPs' role again here is to help our clients find that elusive company with the right culture to support them.

Summary

Understanding your, or your client's, rights at work is an integral part of career management. The law doesn't solve all issues, but it can help you set boundaries, make informed decisions, and hold employers to account. And you don't need to be a legal expert to make use of them. Laws, along with individual company policies and culture, can be tools to help individuals get the treatment at work they deserve.

As HR and careers professionals, our role is not to try and give legal advice. However, having an understanding of some of the basics, and signposting to organisations such as ACAS who can offer free support, will help support clients to thrive in their careers. This is of course relevant to all genders, but for women, already battling with ingrained societal biases, having this knowledge of the law is even more crucial to help them thrive in their careers.

Tools

Unlike the other chapters, there aren't so many 'tools' we can use as CDPs in the area of legal work. However, we can help with good coaching questions, assisting clients to understand the challenges ahead of them and to ascertain whether the issues are internal or external (see chapter 5 on imposter thoughts and feelings vs how you're actually treated). So I've laid out some more coaching questions to help with this, and further useful resources to provide more information and/or signposting for your clients, or to explore for your own career management.

Career coaching questions

- What are you assuming about the situation that is holding you back?
- What is the best thing that could happen to you in the next year ... or in this situation?
- What obstacles are you facing? How could you overcome them?
- What's one situation where you wish you had spoken up more clearly, and what held you back?
- How confident are you in understanding your rights at work, and where might you need more clarity?

Negotiation activity

Here is an activity you can run through with clients when they need advice and support on negotiating an acceptable salary.

Step 1: Say to your client – Imagine you've just been offered a job you're excited about, but the salary is lower than expected. The hiring manager says: 'Does that figure work for you?' What do you say next?

Step 2: Ask the client to respond out loud and role play how this could work. Explore these three tactics together (with some suggested phrases you may wish to incorporate):

Pause and pivot

'Thank you for the offer. I'd love to talk a bit more about the salary before I accept.'

This keeps the lines of communication open, showing there is further discussion to be had, but that you are interested.

Use the market

'Based on my research and what I've seen for similar roles, I was expecting something in the £X range. Is there flexibility?'

This grounds the discussion in data and evidence, not emotion.

Show your worth

'Here's the value I bring, and based on that, I believe a salary of £X is appropriate.'

Highlights more personal evidence on what you'll bring to the role and why you're worth what you're asking for.

Step 3: Ask further coaching questions, such as:

- Which phrase felt most comfortable?
- What would help you feel more confident saying it for real?
- Where are the areas that are holding you back here?

You may also like to use this structure/method to help with other difficult, or as I like to call them, critical conversations. These could be any relating to where an individual feels they are being discriminated against. As Charlotte mentions, sometimes these can be solved with a simple conversation, but our role could be to help our client be brave enough to have it.

Useful resources

When it comes to legal matters, if there are issues and they don't improve after initial communication, then there are places you can seek further support and legal advice:

- ACAS (www.acas.org.uk) for free, confidential advice;
- Citizens Advice for local legal clinics;
- A union rep, if you're a member;
- An employment solicitor, many offer a free initial call;
- Legal expenses insurance, which may be included in home or car cover;
- You can often access legal advice – either free or at least with a known/reputable provider via your EAP (Employee Assistance Programme) if you have one – speak to HR if you're not sure whether you do;
- Many professional bodies often offer reduced-fee legal advice, so check out the details of your memberships or, for example, bodies like the CIPD will have free 15-minute legal clinics during their events, which may provide some support.

Chapter 9
Failing to plan is planning to fail

Looking around the gym I smiled to myself with pride at the scene before me. I know Careers Fairs can be controversial but I believe if you prepare correctly, making sure both volunteers and students understand the purpose, it becomes so much more than a freebie gathering exercise. It is often one of the first steps in a young person's development journey.

'Congratulations, you should be very proud, it's a great event!' One of the employer volunteers broke me out of my reverie.

Little did I know at the time, this was *planned happenstance,* in action (Krumboltz et al., 1999). After four happy years in a school carrying out that well-known 'one' role of Careers Leader, Co-ordinator, Mentor, and Advisor all rolled into one, things were getting stale. I loved supporting the future powerhouse women (in this state girls' school) but discussing their careers was making me think of my own. Like so many non-teachers, there was no development plan and I'd plateaued. I'd established a NfER-recognised Year 7–13 programme from scratch, but there were no promotion or salary increase opportunities, and frankly, I was unchallenged and getting bored.

So when I discovered the volunteer was the Head of Talent at his organisation, and they were looking for a Learning & Development specialist, it seemed like fate. Having previously booked a speaker from John Lewis, a senior HR professional, to speak to the students, the seed of L&D had already been sown. Now was a golden opportunity to grab it with both hands.

I often think of that interview when I'm supporting my clients with their career development, particularly with career changers and unconfident women believing they don't have the skills or experience, or that it's just out of date.

Top tips I give them to develop their career and thrive in career change interviews are all tactics I employed.

1. Learn the language – the CIPD (professional body for HR) website became my friend – from skills audits and Career Path Frameworks, to ROIs, I consumed it all, ready to throw it into my interview presentation, hoping I sounded more knowledgeable than I felt.

2. Sell your transferable skills and experience which can be from any part of your career, not necessarily the most recent. In that interview I relied heavily on my PRINCE 2 qualification and project management experience, which I'd gained many years before in a previous role.

3. Craft your message. Many of my clients worry about changing career, coming back after a maternity break, or feeling like a 'jack of all trades'. These are all fine; you just need to know how to spin that to form your story of how you'll add value to their company and therefore why they should hire you.

That's what I did, and it worked! I got the role, doubled my salary overnight, and had a new and exciting job. I passed my three-month probation and then two weeks later it all came crashing down. Being called into a meeting to be told I was part of the 25% of corporate services whose role was being made redundant was *not* part of the plan.

Like many of my clients, I hadn't really planned the earlier stages of my career; it had mostly just happened. Now, for the first time, I felt lost. I was offered outplacement (a support service provided by employers to help former employees transition to new jobs, typically including career coaching, CV writing, and interview preparation). Truth? I found out the company making me redundant only paid the outplacement company if I took up the services. So I took up the services. Redundancy can be a hugely emotive situation and certainly something that knocks your confidence. And women often do not fare well in the world of redundancy. During the COVID-19 pandemic, female redundancy rose by 76% compared to the previous financial crisis, according to analysis by the House of Commons Library (2021), while longer-term trends show that 4.3% of female executives were made redundant compared to 3.2% of male executives, based on data submitted to the House of Commons by the Chartered Management Institute (2013).

Working with my outplacement career coach taught me so many things, and it's no surprise that having gained lots of senior talent and learning development experience from other companies, when I set up my own, outplacement was the first service I wanted to offer. And one of the biggest things it taught me – if you don't have a plan for your career, someone else will plan it for you. There will always be things outside of your control, like redundancy, but having a plan will help you be able to get back on track far quicker and less painfully, if you know what that track is. But contrary to popular opinion, making a development plan doesn't start with the career; it starts with an honest reflection of you.

Where to start with development

Many clients come to me in a rush. Perhaps they've been waiting a long time to be brave enough to make a change, or they're simply a woman trying to 'do it all' and feel like there is no time to lose. They're not sure where they're headed, but they want to get there fast. They've drifted so far, making 'in the moment' decisions, rather than working to a plan. Now they want that plan; they're just not so sure what to put on it. Or for women lacking confidence, maybe they do know; they're just not sure if they're brave enough to voice it.

So often, to move forward, the best thing is to pause. Encourage and support a period of self-reflection (see chapters 6 and 7). Also reviewing career to date, what does that tell the client about what they do/do not want going forward and setting some goals for the future? Only then will they need to reflect on what development they need to get there.

Vision boards

Throughout a lot of my career, if anyone had simply asked 'what do you want for the future?' or 'where do you want to be in five years?', I would have cringed. And many of my clients are the same. The problem is, especially for women, with so many expectations on them from friends, family, children, and society itself, there is too much noise in their own minds to work out what is in their hearts.

A great way to break down this tricky concept of the future is through activities like journaling or making a vision board. This is a creative and visual tool used to help clarify, concentrate, and maintain focus on specific life goals. It typically involves creating a physical or digital collage of images, words, and affirmations that represent what you want to achieve or attract into your life. There are many benefits to taking this approach:

- Helicopter view – enables the client to look at the bigger picture first, and not get derailed by specific goals and how to achieve them, and so on.

- Imagery – lots of data suggests our minds process images faster than text, and they are more easily stored in memory. This means they can have more impactful emotional engagement, recall, and decision-making properties.

- Constraint-based clarity – when there is only so much room on your board, it helps you focus on and choose what really matters the most to you.

- Visualisation – using imagery of where you want to be puts you in the mindset of already being there and visualising what that would be like.

- Reinforcement – whether it's a physical copy or a digital one, I always encourage clients to have it somewhere that they can see it on a regular basis to remind them of that vision for the future. I even take a picture of mine and have it as my phone screensaver.

- Law of attraction – some believe that it helps manifest what you want.

- Ambition – a non-threatening way to talk about dreams for their future, which, as Vanessa Cowland, a People Development Director, points out, can often be tricky in normal situations. 'I'm not sure how liked you are, particularly as a working mum, when you talk with anyone about ambition and where you might dare to be in the future.' This can be a gentle, non-judgemental way for CDPs to help their female clients open up these conversations.

While vision boarding can be used with any client, I've noticed it tends to resonate particularly well with females. Many seem to find the unique combination of imagination, intention, and a feelings-driven approach a holistic style which resonates. It helps them stay inspired and honest about what truly aligns with them.

As well as with individual coaching clients, I've also run CDP-specific vision board sessions at the start of each year, and one group has carried on meeting up to review their progress. Here are the group's thoughts on what they like about it and how it might be useful to use with clients:

1. What do you like about vision boarding?
    - I like that it taps into what lies beneath and how accessing the subconscious can be so powerful. It's fun too!
    - It is a way of pulling together different aspects of your life into your thinking and planning.
    - I had not done a vision board before, and I really enjoyed being creative.

2. How do you find it impacts on your career, or does it?
    - It reminds me to follow the things that are important to me and helps me check in when I'm doing them that this is my vision.
    - My vision board has been something I have referred back to – am I making progress with this? Is this still important to me? Why has this been tricky to move forward with? So it continues to raise questions for me.
    - Lots of people struggle to talk or write, so a visual way to choose things that appeal is really useful, and then interesting to think about why you chose those pictures.

3. Do you think a vision board could support someone to develop their career confidence? If so, how?
    - 100% yes. It might give someone confidence in their agency and ability to change and influence future direction and steps. Reminds someone it's their masterpiece and to enjoy the journey, intentionally.
    - Definitely. I have used the concept with several of my customers and it is endlessly fascinating to see the different interpretations. I have seen it used as a way to consider the lifestyle changes that could take place alongside a new job. I have also seen it used as a way to align practical and emotional aspects of life and identify solutions. Those who have used it report back the value of seeing their thinking visually represented.
    - I would recommend it as a relaxed way to engage with a client and start a conversation.

4. Would you give any recommendations/top tips for someone working on a vision board – either of their own, or tips for helping a client do theirs?
    - Don't overthink it. Trust in the process. Treat it as a self-care exercise – a space just to be.

- Customers often feel uncomfortable with the lack of guidance at the beginning, and all recognise the value of being 'allowed' to represent their ideas in their own style by the end! So I simply offer reassurance and encouragement at the outset. The conversations raised by the end product are always fruitful, so I would encourage discussion.

5. Any time you wouldn't recommend using a vision board with a client?
   - When the client doesn't want to or doesn't feel ready.
   - I always give customers a choice whether to do this activity, and I give examples of styles I have previously seen, but encourage them to choose their own approach.

See the Tools section for instructions on how to create a vision board.

Goals

Once you have that vision, the next step is to build some tangible goals around it, before then being able to understand your development needs. And I know, some of you, and your female clients, just sagged when I mentioned goals. For women in particular, they have a lot of noise from the media about how they 'should' live their lives; they have endless 'to-do' lists (not just their own, but taking on that of family members, children, friends, co-workers – the lists are endless). So the thought of setting some goals and even linking that to development feels like just another thing that needs to be done.

But here's the thing … that means those goals that are floating around in their minds aren't exciting enough. They're not big enough, or challenging enough, or maybe they feel too big right now. That's OK, CDPs can help break them down into something more manageable. But, and I cannot stress this enough, those goals really need to excite and engage your client; they need to put real fire in their belly. And if they don't, it's time to go back through this book and work out what's going on. Are they a representation of someone else's idea of success? Do they not align to their values? Or are they currently worded in such a way that they feel negative rather than exciting? Turning negative statements, for example, 'I want to work somewhere I'm not ignored for being a woman' needs to become something positive and inspiring, such as 'I am keen to work for a values-led company that treats everyone as individuals'.

Once we've got goals which give nervously excited butterflies, the next step is to word it in such a way that it does actually feel achievable and helps the client see where gaps are which need to be filled by development. To do this, it's helpful to frame them in a SMART way. While SMART ensures objectives are Specific, Measurable, Achievable, Relevant, and Time-bound, NLP (Neuro-Linguistic Programming) approaches can make them smarter, by helping to test how well formed the goal truly is. Ask: Is the goal stated in the positive? Focusing on what you want rather than what you're avoiding creates motivation. Is the goal within the person's control? If it depends too much on others, it can lead to frustration. Is it clearly defined? Make sure the language is unambiguous and practical. What will be the evidence that it's been achieved? Define the sensory cues – what will you see, hear, or feel when the goal is accomplished? What resources do you already have, and what will you need? This builds realism and confidence. Combining SMART with NLP can lead to goals that are not only structured but also emotionally engaging, personally relevant, and more likely to succeed.

Great questions to ask here include:

- What is important to you about this?
- How will you know when you've achieved it?

Even with great goals, however, which can be motivating in themselves, they can still feel daunting. Using NLP techniques here, encouraging the client to imagine themselves as having already achieved that goal, and then working their way backwards, is a useful technique. It's like learning to drive a car. Just backwards. Imagine your final destination, then reverse backwards. Development will give you that map to help you to reverse and go forward, so it is essential for career management and getting to where you want to be.

Development plans

And the best way of describing that 'map' is to have a development plan. There are lots of formats and ways of doing this (see the Tools section for further information) but really what it looks like doesn't matter so much, as long as it works for you. It's just important to *have* one. Vanessa adds that to be effective, a development plan 'needs to have a sense of ambition, and needs to be linked to what gives you energy, what puts you in flow'.

For CDPs, it's crucial to ensure our female clients aren't holding themselves back, to think ambitiously and design the life they truly want. The traditional career ladder is long gone, but we rarely discuss what replaces it. This can leave people feeling lost. But no ladder doesn't mean no progress. Today, individuals have more control than ever to shape their careers, inside or outside their organisation. I often describe it as a career climbing frame; multiple routes, not just one, and a development plan helps prepare for the tougher climbs.

The earlier you start that preparation, even before you're fully ready, the more effective it will be. As Vanessa puts it: 'Development plans often get a bad reputation as they focus on the gaps and miss out the strengths. Your plan should be a mixture, of both the gaps and building on those strengths, on things that get you excited.'

What holds women back from development plans

As a Learning & Development professional (as well as RCDP), I've often seen a lack of development plans, particularly for women. The reasons for this include:

- Reticence: Many fear that asking for development signals they're not good enough, especially hard for women who often struggle with perfectionism. But development isn't about fixing flaws; it's about growing from good to great, whether by building strengths or tackling blind spots.

- Ownership: Some assume development should come from the manager. But as Vanessa says, 'They're not in your head, and they don't really know what gives you flow, what brings joy at work.' It starts with the individual; managers can support with everything from budget to approvals, but they can't lead your development for you.

- Time: Time is a common barrier, especially when development is seen only as formal training. Vanessa notes that for women particularly, 'time for themselves is limited, they're spreading themselves thinly and therefore thinking about development is part of that squeeze'. Working with CDPs is a quick, effective way to take some time out quickly yet powerfully and work out a plan for moving forward sustainably.

- Energy: Development planning should consider natural energy cycles, such as previously mentioned in chapter 2 regarding hormones. As

Emma Jones says, hormonal changes can impact capacity, 'from a development perspective, with hormonal things that might be happening, sometimes it's about going for a safer option if that's what you need'. That's OK, what matters is staying intentional and using the ebbs and flows of your energy as part of your strategic plans to get the most out of you and your career development.

- Imagination: Development isn't just training. Stretch projects, shadowing, or stepping outside your usual role can be just as powerful, and often more relevant to real growth.

Additional challenges

Ageism

For those developing early in their careers, just getting a foot in the door can feel like a huge hurdle, especially in a job market that feels sparse. As Farrah Morgan puts it, 'The stakes feel very high, the job market feels very scarce.'

In a digital world where mistakes feel permanent and public, many are holding back. 'A lot of people are self-rejecting, not trusting their gut, not putting themselves out there at scale … it's an attitude gap as much as a knowledge one,' Farrah explains. Fear of being judged, especially among digital natives raised on performance and perfection, can make even trying feel too risky, 'where everything is viewed, recorded, judged, and permanently available for their mistakes to be viewed'.

This fear of failure is something employers frequently raise, especially with younger candidates who seem hesitant to take chances. Farrah, like many career professionals, focuses just as much on confidence building as on practical steps. And there is hope. 'Once Gen Z start their careers, they want to hit the ground running,' she says. 'And to be honest, I actually notice the female candidates do better, some of the best places I've helped grads get into have been female, they tend to do very well when they're motivated or feel empowered.' Many are simply looking for a clear path to grow and make up for lost time post-COVID.

For those returning after a break, or just generally later in their career, there can be challenges too. As Elizabeth Willetts points out, 'There is often that ageism for women, where employers think their skills aren't as sharp or as relevant, so they get overlooked again.' So whether you have a client returning after a break to have children, or simply are in their 40s or 50s and have been made redundant, helping them to build a development plan, which they can use to show they are keeping their skills relevant, and have a plan for moving forward in their careers, is a crucial activity. It shows they're still keen and interested, with ambition and the skills to match.

Management and leadership

Management and leadership seem like a natural progression for many, but this can be particularly tough for women, especially moving from manager to more senior leadership. Vanessa believes that 'it can be harder for women to set up development conversations, talking about wanting your manager's job'.

One of the key parts of a development plan, particularly for those looking at more senior positions, then, is about the people who can help move them forward, beyond just their manager. Networking is crucial, and Vanessa agrees, 'It's really important to network, and learn how to, because so much about what we want to learn comes from hearing from others' experience.' And with so few women in leadership, it's even more important that those who are pay it forward and help others in this way (more on that in chapter 10).

As CDPs, we can help clients build stronger internal and external networks, a key foundation for their development. This might include using LinkedIn more effectively, attending women-focused networking events, or simply asking someone they admire for an hour of their time. Many women hesitate to reach out, feeling they shouldn't bother others, a mindset shaped by social conditioning and overloaded schedules. But it's not about being a burden; it's about valuing their own development. CDPs can play a vital role in shifting that mindset and encouraging confident, purposeful connection.

As well as CDPs, clients also need to ask: 'Who else can help me achieve my development plan? Who can remove blockers, approve budgets, or connect me with the right people?' Think about how best to engage them.

Vanessa shares a few further top tips on this, including:

- Use accountability partners – not just your manager but peers, friends, or family to keep you on track.

- Write it down in a way that inspires you – use mind maps, Post-its, or anything that helps bring your plan to life.
- Engage your line manager – don't rely solely on them, but do schedule time to talk about your long- and short-term goals, away from day-to-day tasks.

A 70/20/10 approach

Networking is just one piece of the puzzle; there are also lots of other ways to develop beyond formal training. Think about the 70/20/10 approach: 70% of learning comes from on-the-job experiences, 20% from learning through others, and just 10% from formal training. So getting involved in new projects, shadowing colleagues, or finding a mentor can be just as powerful. That said, if training is what you need, don't wait to be offered it – ask. Be clear about the value it will bring to you and the business, and position it as a smart investment in your growth and the organisation's.

How to measure it

To know if development has really worked, you need to plan how you'll measure it *before* you begin. It's not just about ticking boxes on a training evaluation; it's about the real impact on your growth and career. Tracking this progress helps you demonstrate ROI (return on investment) to your employer, showing their investment was worthwhile and positioning you as someone who's committed, capable, and growing within the organisation. It's also a valuable check-in for yourself, to ensure your development is genuinely helping you move towards the goals that matter to you.

CDPs can support clients by asking:

- How will you know it's been successful?
- What will you track to measure progress?
- Who will hold you accountable?
- Who will you celebrate with?

It's important that clients measure their development against what they actually want, not what social media or outside pressures suggest. As Farrah puts it: 'A lot of Gen Z are swept up in the idea of being an entrepreneur or CEO, or juggling a nine-to-five with a side hustle. There's pressure online that traditional jobs mean failure, and I see a lot of anxiety: "Why don't I have a side hustle?" Many aren't ready yet, and that's okay, but they feel like they should be.'

Sometimes, success also means recognising when it's time to move on. For many women, leaving a job can feel like failure, triggering the usual *should*; I should've spoken up, I should be happier, I should've got that promotion. But not every mismatch is your fault. It could be culture, poor management, or just the wrong fit. Even when things *should* be great, they might not be right for you. And that's OK. Sometimes the best measure of growth is having the clarity and confidence to take the next step – somewhere else.

Summary

Failing to plan is planning to fail, and if your client wants to succeed in their career, then having a development plan is crucial. This needs to be steered by them, even if they do have to get eventual line manager buy-in. It should focus on their strengths and build those further, as much as plugging any gaps in skills, knowledge, or experience.

Their company may have a set document/tool to do this, and there may be parts of their longer-term development they don't want to share, so just keep a record of that too. Make sure it's inspiring and engaging, linked to big, exciting goals and their vision for the future. In order to get there, encourage them to think about all the ways they can develop, beyond a traditional classroom-style training course.

Tools

Coaching questions

- Where are you in your life now? Where do you want to get to? What/ who do you need to get you there?
- What are three key dreams you want to achieve? How will you get there?
- Imagine you have achieved your goals. Looking back, what steps did you take to get there?

- How will you measure success?
- Would you be happy in one year's time if your life was the same as it is now?

Creating a vision board

Step 1: Gather your supplies: magazines, glue, scissors, and so on. If doing digitally, try to gather some links to where you're looking for pictures; don't start selecting yet.

Step 2: Create an inspiring space. Remove the clutter, choose some gentle background music or keep it quiet if you prefer, and light a nice candle.

Step 3: When working with clients, I reassure them that it is not about artistic skills; it's simply another way to help them self-reflect and think about what they want out of life. I also often start by doing some journaling – asking them to reflect back on the previous year/period of time, questions such as:

- What were you most proud of?
- What was the greatest feeling you had?
- What was your why?

And then ask them to think ahead for the next year:

- What would you do this year if you weren't afraid? Could you?
- What do you want to learn this year?
- How will you achieve your vision – who might you need help from, what resources, and so on? What habits fuel your confidence?

Step 4: Start collecting pictures. I encourage the clients at this stage not to be too selective; we're not worrying about what goes on the board at this stage, just pick out pictures which 'speak' to them. Give them a set time for this. At the end, ask them if they're comfortable sharing some pictures with you and talking about why they might represent their future interests this year.

Step 5: Make the vision board. Ask the client to start playing, choosing a layout that works for them, and give them a time limit to do this. You can use this finished product as a further coaching tool if you wish. I also often review it with longer-term clients throughout the year. Encourage them not to use it as a stick to beat themselves with; however, it's not a 'to do' list; it's about your vision, and if that changes, or is delayed, that's OK; there's lots you can learn from that.

Assessing development

Individuals often look to their managers for development structure, as they just don't know what they want. Carrying out all the activities in this book will help make them more self-aware and give them a greater understanding of their future career plans. And their development should naturally align with this. However, if they're still struggling, you can coach them through the following model, to help them assess what development they may need to carry out for both now and the future.

What my job needs now (that I'm good at)	What my job needs now (that I'm not so good at)	What my job needs for the future (skills and experience I already have)	What my job needs for the future (skills and experience I'll need to develop)	What I want from a future career (noting where I already have skills/ experience/ confidence and competence vs where I need to develop)

This table is available as part of the online resources that accompany this book. To access, scan the QR code or visit the web address at the start of this book.

(N.B. if you're working with a student, you can use examples of skills, and so on from student life and ask them to think about immediate job interests, either part-time work they're doing, or where they'd like to start in their career vs longer-term prospects.)

Scaling

Development is also a work in progress. Using this coaching technique can help clients work out the mini steps they need to make progress.

The scaling technique is a simple yet powerful coaching tool used to help clients assess their current situation, clarify goals, and track progress over time. You ask the client to rate something, like confidence, motivation, stress, or satisfaction, on a scale from 1 to 10, where 1 is the lowest and 10 is the ideal. Importantly, the scale starts at 1, not 0, because no one is ever truly at zero; there's always something, however small, that's working or keeping them going.

Once the client chooses a number, explore it with questions like: Why that number? What makes it not lower or higher? What's already helping you stay at that level? Then ask, What would make it just one point higher? This builds awareness of both strengths and opportunities for growth.

You can also ask where they'd like to be in, say, six months: What number would feel realistic and meaningful? From there, explore: What would need to happen to get closer to that number? What support, habits, or actions would help? What's one small step you could take this week? This keeps goals grounded, progress measurable, and momentum building.

What is your level of confidence?

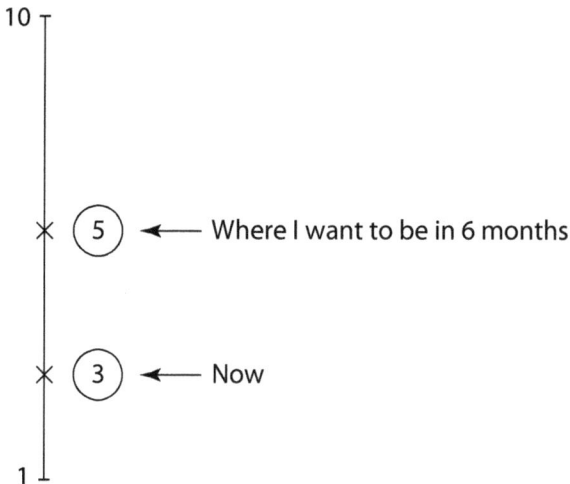

10

×　⑤　◄――― Where I want to be in 6 months

×　③　◄――― Now

1

Chapter 10
Legacy

Growing up in the 1980s, weekends meant a few key things. Bruce Forsyth's *Generation Game* on Friday nights (cue the cries of 'And a cuddly toy!', if you know, you know), followed by Saturdays filled with *The Dukes of Hazzard*, burgers for lunch, and, on one memorable occasion, a torn ankle ligament from cartwheels outside. Why? Because Dad was in charge. Saturdays were Mum's working days, doing accounts for a local baby shop.

I used to visit her; posh prams on the shop floor, great cakes in the café, but the best bit was heading down to the office where Mum worked. It was piled high with paperwork and wasn't much more than a cupboard; sounds familiar to most of us working in careers! But that tiny space was one of my first experiences of the world of work.

Dad, meanwhile, was a warehouse manager, first at the famous Rocking Horse Company, later at a lighting firm where I rode the forklift (health and safety be damned!) His jobs always felt exciting, but I was equally impressed by Mum. Even then, I understood she was doing something for herself, and for us. At a time when women faced real barriers to progress, she was raising three daughters *and* working. I never begrudged her absence; I felt proud.

It's why I've never questioned working women; it was a given that I'd have a career. And with such a strong role model, it's no surprise my sisters and I have each had interesting, varied careers. That's Mum's legacy, whether she planned it that way or not.

I chose not to have children, so I've often thought about what *my* legacy might be. I hope this book forms part of it, alongside the work I do with clients and in the wider careers profession. But it got me thinking: why is legacy, especially for women, so important?

History lives on

We come full circle here, as the impact of history which we looked at in chapter 1, sadly still lives on. Progress has been made, but as International Women's Day (IWD) 2025 showed, we're still a long way from full gender parity. Whether it's high-level misogyny in politics and social media, at macro level, or manifesting at micro level, it all impacts women's confidence. And make no mistake, there is a clear connection between things happening at macro and micro levels. As Jo Phillips puts it, 'Every single time a female stands up for herself, she stands up for every female.' Which very neatly links to the 2026 IWD theme of give to gain and the idea that when women thrive, we all rise. Which is what this chapter is all about!

However, for some, as we've explored, it can be easier said than done. Vicki Knights highlights that 'many women come with a fear of being visible, using their voices, as they don't want to be judged'. So CDPs can help here by creating a safe space where women can be honest about the things that they find hard when it comes to showing up and being visible in the workplace without worrying about being judged and then supporting them with how to overcome this. For Jo, encouraging women to use their voice is indeed crucial. Jo says, 'Just use your voice. Some will like it, others won't. Ultimately worrying about what people do or don't think is a waste of emotional energy. If you are using your voice for good, if you are standing up for what you believe, and if you are following your path, use your voice.'

CDPs can further support this, as our role is to encourage clients to understand they are perfectly them, and that's someone the world needs to see and hear. Lee Gilbert also agrees that helping someone understand 'who you truly are, showing up as your personal brand, is a really powerful thing. It helps a degree of acceptance for them, and that's a beginning part of most things in life but then equipping them with the skills for showing up, and what that looks like for them, is something else.'

And the more we can hold that space of psychological safety and non-judgement, to help individual women to be brave, to develop their brand, and to make it visible to others, the more they will also feel it's OK to share theirs. It's part of the power and the privilege of the work we do; it has a far greater reach than we often realise, or talk about.

Hopefully, some of the activities throughout this book have encouraged greater strength for women in doing this. Not just for women themselves but for all humans to be allies to the cause, as making things better for women is making things better for everyone. And to that end, we need to keep ensuring men are part of this, as we all work together. Whether you're working with a female client or just generally participating in society, make this better. Vicki agrees, saying that 'it's really important to bring men to the table as well. Because if we solely create women-only spaces, men miss out on hearing the conversations we're having and understanding what we're going through.'

Women supporting women?

Now, given that at times it feels like the whole world is against us, you'd be forgiven for thinking women always show up and support other women. But sadly, you'd be wrong. Many of the women I spoke to have experienced challenges with other women, from probing and intrusive questions about disability, to unsupportive female managers, to women walking over each other to get to the top. And as Mo (Mousumi) Kanjilal highlights, 'Just because someone is similar to you doesn't necessarily mean they'll behave as you want, so look for your allies.'

I've had similar situations, often at women-only networking groups who automatically assume I am also a mother. I've learned over the years to take this on the chin, to not be offended by either the assumption, or the endless questions or tumbleweed when they realise I'm not; but I shouldn't have to. We can all do better to be inclusive of all women, whatever their personal circumstances. Lucy Marie Hornsby suggests a solution to this is to 'come at things from a place of curiosity, asking questions rather than just making assumptions, whatever the topic at hand'.

As CDPs we can support our clients with mapping this out, finding out where their tribe, where their allies, might be lurking. It's not as simple as saying other women will be their tribe; however, Vicki also recognises the value of women-only spaces, adding that 'women can feel like they're pitted against each other, but we need to lift each other up, and often female-only safe spaces help women realise they're not alone'.

So they shouldn't be discounted out of hand. Other options like finding groups where you might be able to feel that sense of belonging, like a group for women of colour or for mums or non-mums, or even professional bodies in the sector you work, can all be useful places to explore.

Beating sector stereotypes

We can also all play a part in helping to break down stereotypes, as these can create confidence issues for women, starting early in life. And as Katherine Jennick points out, 'It's great that there is more careers work now happening in primary schools, but other things can also be done. I heard on the radio recently a reference to police*men*. A gender-neutral term could have been used, it's that simple.'

Indeed, those of us of a certain age may remember those adverts for a brand of chocolate bars and their slogan: 'It's not for girls.' More 'banter' that actually did harm, and probably wouldn't pass marketing standards now. But in real life, are there women still battling the desire for a career in sectors which are still seen as 'not for girls'?

Research suggests that gender stereotypes are formed as early as age seven and can significantly influence children's career choices (Tipton, 2018). This isn't just about which sectors are seen as 'suitable' for each gender, but the deeper messaging behind it. Girls are often encouraged to be quiet, keep small, and be appearance-focused, while boys are told to hide their emotions. These early messages can affect not only mental health but also the career paths young people feel are open to them.

Victoria Collins, Director of a construction company, says in construction and engineering it has traditionally been seen as a 'man's world' where when she started out at 14, half-naked pictures of women pinned-up were the norm, and her Dad wouldn't even let her use the site toilet because it was so disgusting. Vanessa Cowland meanwhile found the female apprentices at an engineering firm she previously worked at were getting changed in the car, as nobody had thought to put in a female toilet.

Despite the history, however, women can (and do) have very successful careers in sectors like manufacturing, engineering, construction, and all the trades. As Victoria points out, success in a career should not be about gender but your 'personal values, passions, and skills. It's not about fitting the mould, but that can knock your confidence when you don't feel like you do, unless more of us speak out against this'.

Thankfully, times do seem to be changing and Victoria agreed, noting the dramatic changes in construction, where women are starting to be welcomed. Ruth Forster also noted a huge shift in these traditionally male-dominated sectors and believes this is in part down to the work being done in education. 'When I do voluntary work in education, I see the shift in the equality in programmes being offered, all career options are discussed with all genders, I want to give them praise for not putting people in boxes.'

CDPs can play a huge part here, ensuring young people in particular, but even women who are looking to change career understand all the options open to them. Not just by sector, but the particular roles within it. We can also support clients with advocating for themselves, as Farrah Morgan points out that with Gen Z 'a hyper masculine environment can be that which puts them off staying longer'. Likewise, Ruth also highlighted the challenges in these sectors which can impact women more, such as the disconnect between family life and shift patterns. And Victoria discussed the need for resilience in industries like construction where 'mental health struggles are high, with tragically around two construction workers a day taking their own lives in the UK alone'. There is much support CDPs can do to help in all these areas, from education to identifying skills and interests to establishing resilience plans. We can also encourage women in those sectors to ensure they are visible, an inspiration to future generations.

Career transition hurdles still to overcome

It's also important to recognise the challenges women face at key points of transition, from early career to returning after maternity leave, or stepping into leadership roles. There are many ways CDPs and HR can help and encourage females to do the same. Each stage brings barriers that require thoughtful, tailored support.

Young women

Young women in the workplace may face:

- Gender and age bias: Nearly half of women in their 20s report career setbacks due to ageism (Fair Play Talks, 2022).
- Unconscious bias: Younger women often face assumptions based on appearance or perceived inexperience.

- Pressure to find meaningful work: Gen Z often seek purpose-driven careers, which can be difficult to align with the realities of the job market.

- High expectations: This generation tends to be ambitious, especially around salary and progression, sometimes leading to frustration or job-hopping.

- Confidence disconnect: Some young women feel they should be further ahead, which can affect their self-esteem or cause blame towards employers. The reality is often somewhere in between. CDPs can support clients to realistically assess their skills, build development plans, and benchmark salaries to create more grounded career strategies.

According to research from the Young Women's Trust, 42% of young women said they wouldn't know how to ask for a promotion or pay rise, compared to just 28% of men (Young Women's Trust, 2024). This highlights that getting in the door isn't the only barrier. Progressing into leadership roles is still a major hurdle.

So many of these challenges can be addressed by women as much as men. We can pave the way for future generations, but does this always happen? Simple answer: 'no'. As Jo points out, 'Women all over the globe have experienced "queen bee" syndrome, where a woman has fought so hard to get where she is, she creates barriers and unnecessary stress for other women.' However, once again, this is the responsibility of us all to create a better environment where women don't have to fight so hard, where they support each other to help lift them up and let them shine.

Women in leadership

Supporting women in leadership roles is another way we can make things better for everyone, both now and in the future. Mo reflected on working in senior leadership where 'nobody expected me to be there, I had to fight harder, outsell everyone and stand up for myself but was then labelled as aggressive and bossy, for trying to claim my place'. When you're one of five to ten women in a leadership team of hundreds, as was Mo's case, with only one woman (usually an HR Director) at the next level, it can be tough.

So how can we help women achieve leadership roles for themselves, and help others to get there? One of the ways to achieve that is by all leaders showing up with emotional intelligence, creating psychological safety, and being authentic and vulnerable. In a session with a CDP, while we can't force these behaviours on a client, we can support them to become more self-aware and confident in their own self and show up as who they really are. This is all part of career management. And Jo agrees, the impact for women in particular knowing these things is huge. 'My key advice would be to know your worth, in every scenario, show up as your authentic self, and hold the space that is rightfully yours. You are not in competition with other women; you are setting the example for the next generation. Keep them in mind when you act, when you speak, and when you show up.'

Despite the challenges, there are signs of progress. As of 2024, 42.8% of FTSE 100 directorships are now held by women, and around half of all new appointments are women (House of Commons Library, 2024). These figures show real momentum, and it's important for CDPs to highlight both the ongoing challenges and the opportunities available. Too much focus on the barriers can overwhelm clients. We must empower, uplift, and support women to see what's possible.

The lack of role models is real, but it's not insurmountable. CDPs can support young women by helping them develop their voice, whether that's expressing their needs, building confidence, or asking for flexible working arrangements in leadership roles. Encouraging clients to craft clear messaging around these asks is crucial.

CDPs also play an important role in supporting those already on the path to leadership by:

- Helping clients identify and articulate their leadership strengths.
- Coaching them to navigate office politics, conflict, and visibility with confidence.
- Supporting the development of leadership CVs, interview prep, and personal branding.
- Encouraging networking, mentoring, and sponsorship opportunities.
- Normalising the challenges and reinforcing that leadership comes in many styles and not just the dominant (often male) model.

Whether it's a woman just starting out or one aiming for the boardroom, CDPs have a powerful role to play in ensuring gender doesn't limit their career growth.

Showing up for others

There are many ways that women can support themselves as women and help future generations. These can include having and delivering coaching, mentoring, and sponsorship. Again, this links to a consistent conversation I have with clients about finding their tribe. Working out who their support network are, who could help them in a plethora of ways. From people they seek out when they're feeling down, who help lift them up, to the ones whose wisdom and counsel they seek for advice. There are specialists (including CDPs) who would be sought over particular scenarios or those who are inspirational; they're where the client wants to be one day and could show a potential path.

These conversations often come up in the very early contracting stages, where we talk about guidance, advice, coaching, mentoring, and what these nuances even mean. But I often find it re-enters the conversation, particularly with women. Whether that's down to all the areas we've discussed throughout the book, the instances of being marginalised, moving up the ranks and seeing fewer 'people like me', or the fact we're so used to doing it all ourselves, I don't know. But one thing is clear: women are often keen to connect with others, to learn, develop, and grow, as well as seeking support. Coaching offers a great way to empower women to understand themselves and their own path. And once that path has been established, or simply part of the journey to it, seeking out a mentor can be a great way for women to add extra fuel to the fire burning in their bellies.

But as well as being mentored can be useful for one's career, mentoring others can also be useful (through reverse mentoring) and a tangible, practical way to create a legacy and support other women. As Jo puts it, 'We need more women at the top who are their genuine authentic selves, who will pull other women up as they rise, who will put their hand out and pull them up, and the next pulls up the next and together we all get there. My key advice would be to know your worth, in every scenario, show up as your authentic self, and hold the space that is rightfully yours. You are not in competition with other women; you are setting the example for the next generation. Keep them in mind when you act, when you speak, and when you show up.'

Mentorship

I asked many of the women I interviewed what actually makes a good mentor, and the feedback was pretty unanimous. It usually doesn't matter who it is; they don't necessarily need to be the same as you; they just need to be good at mentoring or have some useful information and advice to impart. As Kate Nash put it, 'Sometimes you want to surround yourself with sassy powerful women who take no prisoners, sometimes it's an issue-based piece of advice you need.'

And for Lee and Lucy Marie, they felt allyship was at the core. As Lee explained, for a young trans woman, 'any ally is a good mentor, regardless, because you can mentor people on knowledge, skill, and behaviour without lived experience'. She does, however, believe that as a trans woman, it is her 'responsibility to pay back to the trans community, through mentoring others, for all those who have treaded the journey ahead of me, but I don't think it's a prerequisite for a mentor to have lived experience as it depends what you're mentoring on'. For Lucy Marie meanwhile, she doesn't believe that gender is crucial: 'probably about 90% of my cheerleaders, mentors, allies, have been men. That might be down to the industry I work in, but the point is, I think mentoring is about the person.'

Ruth Forster also agreed that it's not so much about gender as it is about choosing someone to match your 'personal circumstances and what you need. I've always had coaches and I've always picked them based on their expertise not whether they are male or female. Also not about any woman, has to be the *right* woman.' And Ruth also voiced her frustrations that people complain or say what young people need, when 'if everyone just gave one hour to go and support young people, we'd be in a whole different place. I am also a big believer in reverse mentoring. We have so much we can learn from each other.'

Vanessa also agreed, saying that it's about 'if you feel that synergy in terms of communication style and someone you can be vulnerable about your development areas quite quickly, is going to be the best mentor for you'. However, Vanessa also highlighted that many women being asked to mentor others might just feel like another thing on the to-do list. 'My sense is that many women can't be flattered into this, like many men could be, you need to sell more about the impact it could make on the mentee, and the difference just one hour could make to them.' And Kate also pointed out that if you do ask, 'the worst that can happen is they say no. Women sometimes feel like they have to know all the answers. But asking for the advice and support of others is the most liberating thing we can do to get us to the next step.'

Of course, discussing with clients the idea of being mentored or completing mentoring will, in part, be down to where they are in their career. For those starting out, they may be more focused on developing the skills and getting on with their own career before learning from others. However, moving back to the idea of allyship is perhaps an even more important point of sponsorship.

At any stage in our career, we can support women, whoever we are, by acting as their ally or sponsor. Mo highlights that this has been 'proven to be such an important thing for helping people progress with their careers because you need someone to talk to and sound things out with. You need somebody who can suggest different things you could do, or to introduce you to people and champion you, speak up about you when they're in meetings that you're not in, or even defend you if needed.' Whether you see them as a mentor or a sponsor, she also points out that it's important they have the right connections and can introduce you to people who will help you go further in your career.

As well as individual support, Vanessa also suggests the benefits of group networks, such as women's networks. She gives the example of a previous company where she helped establish such a network, where they had everything from speakers to lobbying and campaigning for particular things within the organisation.

Whether it's one-to-one or in a group setting, there are so many things that women can get involved with to boost their own career and support other women to do the same. The future is bright if we all work together with our allies to make real and lasting change.

Summary

Both in this chapter and throughout the book, we've looked at ways as CDPs and individuals on our own career journeys, we can create confidence and build paths to career success. There are many ways you can do this, not just for yourself, but clearing the path for others as well, including:

1. Lift as you climb – and cheer loudly.
    Make it your mission to bring other women with you by offering encouragement, sponsorship, and real feedback to help them move forward as their authentic selves.

2. Be the voice that says, 'You can do this.'
    Often, women hold back from applying, speaking up, or leading. Be that person who encourages them to go for it and not be held back by their inner critic.

3. Create opportunities that stretch and strengthen.
    Give women the chance to lead projects, speak at events, or take on stretch roles, even before they feel 100% ready.

4. Normalise ambition and self-belief.
    Show that ambition and humility can co-exist. Talk openly about your goals and how you overcame imposter feelings along the way, or better yet, kick that Imposter Monster into touch and show everyone how confident you are and they can be.

5. Be transparent about your journey.
    Share your missteps and learning moments. Help others see that confidence isn't a constant or straight line, it's built through risk, resilience, reflection, and ongoing work, including learning through so-called 'failure'.

6. Sponsor boldly, not just quietly.
    Don't just mentor, advocate for women when they're not in the room, whatever your own gender. Recommend them for promotions, high-visibility work, and leadership roles.

7. Model boundaries and self-worth.
    Demonstrate how to negotiate, advocate, and set boundaries. Instead of feeling guilty about this, know that you're giving other women to advocate for themselves too.

8. Build confidence into the culture.
   Encourage feedback that builds capability and confidence, with clear goals and not just focused on behaviours for women. Encourage development practices, for you and others, and know that learning and growing is not a sign of weakness, but growth.

9. Challenge the systems that undermine confidence.
   Speak up about unequal standards and exclusionary practices, even when they're unintentional. Make sure they are inclusive of all staff, including all women, and that they don't make them question their worth.

10. Be the legacy, not just the leader.
    Make it your legacy to leave behind women who believe in themselves more than they did before they met you. Remember that confidence is contagious, pass it on and always encourage it in others. Lift others up; don't be threatened by them.

And as CDPs, ensure all your clients are living and breathing these ten top tips, for both themselves and the women they work with. Make it better for everyone.

Tools

Coaching questions

- What or who inspires you? How could you inspire others?
- At the end of your life, how would you like to be remembered?
- It's your retirement party. What are people saying about you and your career? What makes you happy/unhappy about this? Is there anything you would change? What steps could you take to make that happen?
- If you were to meet your younger self for a coffee, what would you say to her?
- What have you learned about yourself that you would be willing to share with others?

Mentoring

As we've established, finding the right mentor for your needs is crucial. A way to help clients do this is to first assess where they're at, where they want to be, and who can help them bridge the gap. The more specific they can be about their needs, the more appropriate a mentor they may be able to find, and the more they may be able to help them.

Step 1: Establishing where they are at now through coaching questions such as:

- What am I working on developing (skills, mindset, network)?
- What challenges or transitions am I currently facing?
- What does 'growth' look like for me over the next 12–18 months?

The goal here is to pinpoint exactly what their focus is that they may need help with.

Step 2: Break it down.
Help the client to list out the types of mentoring they might need in more detail, for example:

- Type of support is confidence building;
- What they need, for example, a better understanding of themselves; and then
- Writing down some ideas of who could possibly mentor them in this area (and assisting with helping them work out who could if they don't know anyone).

Step 3: Focus.
Support the client to work out how/where/when they'll approach the mentor and encourage them to get REALLY specific on what it is they might need. Kate encourages even 'just asking can I have 30 mins of your time, to suit you, I'll buy the coffee and the doughnuts' can still be hugely helpful if you've thought about what it is you want to get out of the conversation.

You can also carry out a similar process if a client is interested in mentoring others, by first identifying specifically what they could mentor on and then who they could reach out to (either individuals who directly may be in need of mentorship, or those who are managing this kind of thing for others, such as those responsible for early talent in their organisations).

Allyship and support

And not so much a tool, but a suggestion. Whether you're working with a client to help reflect, or doing so yourself, take a moment to sit back and think about the situations you've been in from the previous day, week, month, year.

- Where have you been an ally for (other) women?
- Were there moments you could have spoken out but didn't?
- Were there situations you could have helped by offering further advice and support?

Think about the legacy you want to leave and what you can do to support both your own career confidence and that of others. Remember again that making it better for (all) women is making it better for all people, whatever their gender. You don't just have to be a mentor; there are lots of other ways you can support too, from giving advice on particular projects rather than general mentoring to volunteering as a judge for awards supporting women early in their career. There are many ways to get involved and support others.

One final thought ...

And that, my friends, is that. What a journey it has been, interviewing some utterly amazing women (huge thanks again to them all!), taking their fabulous insights and sharing my own. Whether you're a CDP, working in a careers role or HR, or a woman reading this for your own journey, I hope this guide has furnished you with a plethora of useful insights and practical tools to help you move forward. So that all women can shine with the sparkle and confidence they truly deserve.

Because I know we don't always feel that way. I, for one, am often described in certain circles as one of the 'careers titans' or a 'famous careers person', as someone once said. While I'm proud of the work I do – I didn't just get the CDI Career Coach of the Year 2023 award by fluke – I'm also very aware that what you see on social media and what goes on behind the scenes isn't always the same thing. The irony that I've never felt less confident than when I started writing this book, about career confidence, is not lost on me.

And that feeling goes for both men and women who often face challenges. Sometimes that is created by society, sometimes by employers, sometimes our own worst enemy is living between our own two ears. And all of this is about the fact that making it better for women makes it better for everyone. It's just one example of how taking the approach of equity, making a level playing field, which requires understanding and adjustments where needed for particular individuals, benefits everyone. There are so many additional nuances to this including a need for inclusivity for people of colour, trans people, those with disabilities, to name just a few.

And to hark back to my own work and life purpose, you might be wondering what mine is. For me, it's quite simple really. Whether helping individuals directly through one-to-one coaching or group coaching and training, or supporting others in the careers community to help clients better, I want to leave this world a better place than when I arrived.

It's that simple really. That's my legacy. What's yours?

As we end the book here, your story is just starting. Write it well.

References

Introduction

House of Commons Library (2024) *Women and the UK economy.* [Online] Available at: https://commonslibrary.parliament.uk/research-briefings/sn06838/ (Accessed: 30 July 2025).

Chapter 1: Dresses with pockets and a 'Whole Lotta History'

Argyris, C. (1999) *On organizational learning.* 2nd edn. Oxford: Wiley-Blackwell.

The Huntington Library, Art Museum, and Botanical Gardens (n.d.) *Object story: Pair of pockets.* [Online] Available at: https://huntington.org/educators/learning-resources/spotlight/object-story-pair-pockets (Accessed: 30 July 2025).

Young Women's Trust (2024) *A world not designed for us: Annual survey 2024.* [Online] Available at: https://www.youngwomenstrust.org/our-research/a-world-not-designed-for-us-annual-survey-2024 (Accessed: 30 July 2025).

Chapter 2: Our makeup (not the stuff we buy in Boots)

CIPD (2023) *Menstruation and support at work.* London: Chartered Institute of Personnel and Development. Available at: https://www.cipd.org/en/knowledge/reports/menstruation-support-at-work (Accessed: 12 September 2025).

The Menopause Charity (2023) *Understanding the impact of menopause in the workplace.* Available at: https://themenopausecharity.org/ (Accessed: 3 August 2025).

Menopause Support (2023) *Perimenopause: The hidden suicide risk.* Available at: https://menopausesupport.co.uk/?p=15624 (Accessed: 3 August 2025).

Wellbeing of Women (2024) *Menstrual health support still lacking in many workplaces: New report.* Available at: https://www.wellbeingofwomen.org.uk/news/menstrual-health-support-still-lacking-in-many-workplaces-new-report/ (Accessed: 3 August 2025).

Chapter 3: Additional barriers ... or are they?

Fair Play Talks (2022) *People of colour, women & millennials report limited access to professional development.* Available at: https://www.fairplaytalks.com/2022/07 /09/people-of-colour-women-millennials-report-limited-access-to-professional -development/ (Accessed: 8 August 2025).

MyDisabilityJobs (2024) *Neurodiversity in the workplace: Statistics update 2024.* Available at: https://mydisabilityjobs.com/statistics/neurodiversity-in-the -workplace/ (Accessed: 12 September 2025).

Office for National Statistics (ONS) (2023) *The employment of disabled people 2023.* London: Department for Work & Pensions. Available at: https://www.gov.uk/ government/statistics/the-employment-of-disabled-people-2023 (Accessed: 12 September 2025).

Chapter 4: The (non)parent trap

FE News (2018) *How can businesses support new parents as they return to work?* Available at: https://www.fenews.co.uk/skills/88-of-mothers-face-problems-when -returning-to-work/ (Accessed: 7 August 2025).

Office for National Statistics (ONS) (2021) *Families and the labour market, UK: 2021.* Available at: https://www.ons.gov.uk/employmentandlabourmarket/peopleinwork/ employmentandemployeetypes/articles/familiesandthelabourmarketengland/2021 (Accessed: 12 September 2025).

Office for National Statistics (ONS) (2023) *Conceptions in England and Wales: 2021.* Available at: https://www.ons.gov.uk/peoplepopulationandcommunity/birthsdeath sandmarriages/conceptionandfertilityrates/bulletins/conceptionstatistics/2021 (Accessed: 7 August 2025).

ResumeLab (2022) *What's it like being childfree at work?* Available at: https:// resumelab.com/career-advice/childfree-at-work (Accessed: 7 August 2025).

UK Government (2023) *Employment Relations (Flexible Working) Act 2023.* Available at: https://www.legislation.gov.uk/ukpga/2023/33 (Accessed: 7 August 2025).

Resources you could share with clients:

- World Childless Week: www.worldchildlessweek.net
- Ageing Well Without Children: https://www.awwoc.org/
- Happy and Childless: http://www.happyandchildless.co.uk
- The Full Stop Community and Podcast: https://www.thefullstoppod.com
- British Infertility Counselling Association: https://www.bica.net

Chapter 5: The Imposter Monster and other scary tales

Clance, P. R. (1985) *The impostor phenomenon: Overcoming the fear that haunts your success*. Atlanta: Peachtree Publishers.

Mohr, T. S. (2014) Why women don't apply for jobs unless they're 100% qualified. *Harvard Business Review*. Available at: https://hbr.org/2014/08/why-women-dont-apply-for-jobs-unless-theyre-100-qualified (Accessed: 15 June 2025).

Technische Universität München (2022) Women do not apply to 'male-sounding' job postings. Available at: https://www.tum.de/en/news-and-events/all-news/press-releases/details/31440?utm_source=chatgpt.com (Accessed: 12 September 2025).

Verbruggen, M. & De Vos, A. (2020) When people don't realize their career desires: Toward a theory of career inaction. *Academy of Management Review*, 45(2), pp. 376–394. https://doi.org/10.5465/amr.2017.0196.

Chapter 6: What makes you, YOU?

Schein, E. H. (1990) *Career anchors: Discovering your real values*. 3rd ed. San Diego: University Associates.

Chapter 7: What do people say when you walk out the room?

Burn, I. (2023) *Job age discrimination for women starts at least 10 years earlier than for men*. University of Liverpool Management School. Available at: https://www.liverpool.ac.uk/management/blog/research/job-age-discrimination-for-women-starts-at-least-10-years-earlier-than-for-men/ (Accessed: 16 July 2025).

Law, B. & Watts, A.G. (1977) *Schools, careers and community: A study of some approaches to careers education in schools*. London: CIO Publishing for the General Synod Board of Education.

Chapter 8: Know your rights

Mitchell, A.M., Jones, G.B. & Krumboltz, J.D. (1979) *Social learning and career decision making*. Cranston, RI: Carroll Press.

Pregnant Then Screwed & Women In Data®. *74,000 women a year lose their jobs for getting pregnant or for taking maternity leave* (Press release/State of the Nation report, 27 February 2025). Available online: https://pregnantthenscrewed.com /74000-women-a-year-lose-their-jobs-for-getting-pregnant-or-for-taking-maternity -leave/

Chapter 9: Failing to plan is planning to fail

Chartered Management Institute (2013) *Written evidence to the House of Commons Business, Innovation and Skills Committee: Women in the workplace, National Management Salary Survey – XpertHR/CMI.* Available at: https://publications .parliament.uk/pa/cm201314/cmselect/cmbis/342/342vw07.htm (Accessed: 17 August 2025).

House of Commons Library (2021) *How has the coronavirus pandemic affected women in work?* Available at: https://commonslibrary.parliament.uk/how-has-the -coronavirus-pandemic-affected-women-in-work/ (Accessed: 17 August 2025).

Mitchell, K.E., Levin, S.A. & Krumboltz, J.D. (1999) Planned happenstance: Constructing unexpected career opportunities. *Journal of Counseling & Development*, 77(2), pp. 115–124. https://doi.org/10.1002/j.1556-6676.1999.tb02431.x.

Chapter 10: Legacy

Fair Play Talks (2022) *People of colour, women & millennials report limited access to professional development.* Available at: https://www.fairplaytalks.com/2022/07 /09/people-of-colour-women-millennials-report-limited-access-to-professional -development/ (Accessed: 7 August 2025).

House of Commons Library (2024) *Women in parliament and government.* Available at: https://researchbriefings.files.parliament.uk/documents/SN06838/SN06838 .pdf (Accessed: 7 August 2025).

Tipton, M. (2018) An investigation into children's gender stereotypes and the effect they have on children's career aspirations. *The STeP Journal: Student Teacher Perspectives*, 5(1), pp. 50–63. Available at: https://insight.cumbria.ac.uk/id/eprint /4010/ (Accessed: 17 August 2025).

Young Women's Trust (2024) *A world not designed for us – Progression.* Available at: https://research.youngwomenstrust.org/annual-survey-2024/a-world-not -designed-for-us/progression/ (Accessed: 7 August 2025).